Copyright © 2013 by Linda R. Barrett
All Rights Reserved.
Printed in the USA

All rights reserved. No part of this publication may be reproduced or transmitted in any form or by any means without written permission of the author.

Cover design by Linda R. Barrett

At Random Publications
260 Lamar Ave. #302
Pueblo, CO 81004
ISBN 978-0-615-75330-0

Acknowledgments

No matter where you are in your spiritual journey, the word of God is needed at random on a daily basis whether a minute by minute, hour by hour, or day by day, His word helps you through the deepest despair or the most joyous event. All the answers are found in scriptures and his promises will speak to you to carry you through the un-chartered waters. This collection of scriptures, poems, and stories is meant to be used randomly as needed. My prayer is that when you are feeling low, you open this book and find peace and comfort for your situation.

I give many thanks to those who encouraged and discouraged me to help me dig deeper into myself and reach my goal of completing this book. Firstly, I give Glory to God as my biggest encourager and supporter. I said to myself, "Why am I doing this," or, "I can't do this," and God answered "You are doing this for me" and "Yes, you can do it." When my brain was unresponsive, He placed new visions that flowed through my keyboard. Secondly I give thanks to my daughter, Audrey Diane, thank you for your understanding the desires of my life. This book is one of my many legacies for you.

To Henry Gregoire, thank you for allowing me to share how God blessed you one windy day, and Jeff Potter, for your delight of joy you post on Facebook under the alter ego of 'Ranger Jeff', which make me and others laugh out loud, and to Carol Keeter who became one of my earth angels. I am deeply humbled by my many cousins; Mary, Sonya, Linda, Alice, Earnest, Danny and Roy (R.I.P.), who touched my life and have been closer than my brothers and sisters. Your presence in my life, the tears we shared, the laughs, and most of all, the love you all have shown me has brought me to where I am today.

Thirdly, I give thanks to Joel Osteen, who has no idea how much his words of encouragement meant to me. Although I have not seen Joel in many years, his words of wisdom appear daily through electronic media. His words would appear just in time to lift me up. The latest message was, "You are not an accident. God has given you the right gifts, the right talent, the right personality. You have the courage, the strength, the ability you need." To that I say a big Amen, and thank you Jesus for leading me in the writing of this book. Although I am no Bible scholar, these words came from my heart. I pray this book will bless your lives, as much as it has blessed me to write the words within these pages.

Table of Contents

1. I Will Be With You
2. Bitter Is Not Better
3. Motivation
4. Compassion
5. Struggles Of The Butterfly
6. Anxiety
7. Friends
8. Abuse
9. Seasons
10. Grudges
11. Somebody's Watching Me
12. Your Savior Really Does Forgive You
13. Downward Spiral
14. Demonstrate Your Faith
15. God's Voice
16. You Are Valuable
17. Tit For Tat
18. Walk In Obedience
19. Sorrow
20. Happiness
21. Let Your Spirit Shine
22. Sin, Oops I Did It Again
23. Imperfect Perfection
24. Just Say No
25. All Your Needs
26. Go Forth And Be Fruity
27. Broken Hearts
28. Fools Folly
29. Be Cheerful
30. Kiss It And Make It Better
31. Humility
32. Patience
33. Love One Another
34. Quiet My Soul
35. Healing
36. Signs
37. Wrestling With Ourselves
38. The Light Shall Lead The Way
39. Thorn In My Side

40.	Unrealistic Expectations
41.	You're Never Alone
42.	The Lord Gives And Takes
43.	Who Are You?
44.	Soul Mates
45.	An Ordinary Life
46.	God's Love
47.	Discouragement
48.	Anger
49.	Can I Have A Witness
50.	God's Strength
51.	Favor Me
52.	Death
53.	Misty Eyes
54.	Show A Little Kindness
55.	Missing Puzzle Pieces
56.	My Life Has Purpose
57.	Guardian Angels
58.	Loser Or Learner
59.	Peace
60.	Spiritual Blindness, Paul's Quest
61.	Ya Think?
62.	Traveling With Happiness
63.	Who Knew
64.	Ticket To Eternal Life
65.	Awakening
66.	God's Plans
67.	Death Looks Good To Me
68.	Getting Lost In The Word
69.	Do Not Be Distracted
70.	God's Mysteries
71.	Be Still
72.	Harold Be Thy Name?
73.	My Everything
74.	Relationships
75.	Lying
76.	Heart Health
77.	Me Me Me, All About Me
78.	Precious Prayer
79.	In Everything Give Thanks
80.	Believe

81.	Focus
82.	God Is Our Greatest Encourager
83.	Can You Fix This
84.	God Is Love
85.	Encouragement
86.	Tears
87.	Worry
88.	God Is Forever Yours
89.	Don't Give Up
90.	Belonging
91.	Friend Buffet
92.	Prayer
93.	Mean As A Second Language
94.	I Can Only Imagine
95.	The Lord Directs Your Steps
96.	Give It Away
97.	Faith Or Fear
98.	Challenges
99.	Perception And Reality
100.	Lighten My Load
101.	He Loves Me He Loves Me Not
102.	My Constant Companion
103.	Out Of The Dark
104.	Love Your Neighbor
105.	When You Are Spiritually Stuck
106.	Band Aid
107.	Get Right With God
108.	Birds Of A Feather
109.	Don't Be Offended
110.	Why Me
111.	The Object Of Your Affection
112.	Time Management
113.	Blowing In The Wind
114.	Defeat
115.	Hugs
116.	No Boundaries For Blessings
117.	Moving Mountains
118.	Got God?
119.	More Than Enough
120.	Wounded Spirit
121.	Touch Me

122.	What's In A Name
123.	Trust
124.	What's Fair Is Fair
125.	The Yellow Brick Road
126.	Brokenhearted
127.	Fork In The Road
128.	Burning Bridges
129.	Draw Me Close To You
130.	I've Been Robbed
131.	Life Is Like A Merry Go Round
132.	Keeping Grounded
133.	What If…Ye Of Little Faith
134.	Conflict
135.	Investing For The Future
136.	Lean On Me
137.	Walk A Mile In My Heels
138.	The Straight And Narrow
139.	Through The Eyes Of A Child
140.	It Is What It Is
141.	Laughter In Heaven
142.	Trust Me
143.	My Fathers Smorgasbord
144.	Rejoice
145.	Kindness Nourishes The Soul
146.	Thirst For God
147.	Save My Soul
148.	Making God Smile
149.	Victory In Jesus
150.	Count Your Blessings
151.	Broken Dreams
152.	Listen To Me
153.	Something's Wrong
154.	You Are My Hiding Place
155.	Eternity Shores

I Will Be With You

"When you go through deep waters
and great trouble, I will be with you.
When you go through rivers
of difficulty, you will not drown."
Isaiah 43:2 (NLT)

Good morning! Through His Holy Spirit, God promises to be with us always if we just ask him. How great is this promise of safety in all our situations? God is so good to promise us that when we accept him and walk with him, that he will be there beside us. When we accept him as Lord of our lives, he forgives and purifies us on the inside so that he can then reside in us. The key to living this life and the next is to daily experience the power of the presence of almighty God. Have a blessed day....walk in 'sonshine'.

Precious Lord, your promises bring tears to my eyes. You are with us always no matter what the trial or tribulation is. We have assurance that you will not allow us to drown when we feel like we can float no longer. I praise your name and thank you for your loving spirit. Amen.

Bitter Is Not Better

"You wicked people! You twist justice, making it a bitter pill for the poor and oppressed. Righteousness and fair play are meaningless fictions to you."
Amos 5:7 (NLT)

Bitterness of the spirit is a poison that can make a heart harden and ultimately destroy your soul. A lot of times it is caused by jealousy, anger, or resentment toward another person. It will rob you of your joy. Some Christians are not on a level playing field. They befriend you but care very little for you. They will smother you with empty flattery and loving gestures. Then, one day they will speak harshly, intimidate, or blindside you in an effort to hurt your feelings and discredit you in front of others. Never forget Gods grace, simple forgiveness can relieve symptoms of bitterness by simply saying to the other person, " I was wrong, please forgive me for my actions." God is tenderhearted and forgives you, if you are on the receiving end of the bitterness, you should forgive as well.

Motivation

"And I am sure that God, who began the good work within you, will continue his work until it is finally finished on that day when Christ Jesus comes back again."
Philippians 1:6 (NLT)

God knew that as humans we don't always give the support that is needed to others; however He is always there for us to lean on. Encouragement is better than discouragement. Either way you will have motivation to complete your goal. Strength comes in hanging on to the promises. Remember, God is your greatest supporter!! Amen.

Lord God, please provide me with the motivation needed to complete my goals. I am not asking that you remove the trials, instead I simply ask that your will be done in my life. Whatever you want for me is what I want for me. Thanking you in advance for the blessings to come my way and for the present blessings in my life that I don't feel I deserve. Amen.

Compassion

"The unfailing love of the Lord never ends! Great is thy faithfulness; his mercies begin afresh each day."
Lamentations 3:22-23 (NLT)

When we think of someone with a kind heart, we immediately think of compassion. Compassion is two things, an emotion when we are warmed with misfortune for someone, and an action such as being kind and considerate to someone in need. Jesus had great compassion for those around him and he spread the good news about God along with showing them his soft forgiving heart. Compassion will cause your heart to tear when you see someone hurting, or in despair. Something deep in your heart will lead you to respond and love them as God loves you. Make sure your heart is not turned to stone and not able to care for those around you. God wants you to pass the test and be a faithful servant. Spread the love to others and let God's light shine brightly through your words and actions. God is love….and you should be too.

Struggles Of The Butterfly

"Those who become Christians become new persons. They are not the same anymore, for the old life is gone and a new life has begun!"
2 Corinthians 5:17 (NLT)

We delight in the beauty of the butterfly, but rarely admit the changes it has gone through to achieve that beauty. The butterfly struggles, we struggle, every struggle has a purpose. Life is an adventure, do you have the courage to go beyond what you see? If you believe it you can attain it, with God it is achievable. The story of the butterfly is amazing, if someone just cracked open the cocoon and released the butterfly, it would be crippled and it would be unable to fly. In the effort of getting through the tiny cocoon opening, fluid from the body of the butterfly flows into its wings so that it will be ready to fly. Just as the butterfly gains its strength to survive through this challenge, the struggles and challenges in our everyday life, prepare us for the obstacles that lay ahead. God is close by, but he allows us to gain our strength on our own. If God allowed us to go through life without any valleys we would not be strong enough to climb the mountains. God helps us develop our own coping skills so that we can use them to fight our way out of our cocoon.

Anxiety

"Let everyone see that you are considerate in all you do. Remember, the Lord is coming soon. Don't worry about anything; instead, pray about everything. Tell God what you need, and thank him for all he has done."
Philippians 4:5-15 (NLT)

When should I worry and when should I not? The Bible says never worry! What can you actually change by worrying anyway? God knows your every need and is looking behind the scenes to bring peace. Even though our concerns are valid, worry will only muddy up your mind and keep you from thinking straight. When you worry you concentrate more on your woes instead of keeping your focus on God. As Believers we should remain focused on God. He is our strength in time of need.

Thank you Jesus for loving me and watching out for me. I know that although I cannot see you I feel you near me. You calm me when I am worried, and bring a peace that is beyond all understanding. Help me to remember to give all my concerns to you, nothing is too big that you can't handle. Amen.

Friends

"Friendship with the Lord is reserved to those who fear him. With them he shares the secrets of his covenant."
Psalm 25:14 (NLT)

I have many friends who range from casual acquaintances to those who are faithful and would be there rain or shine. Family is close however sometimes friends are closer than those family ties. We share companionship, fellowship, affection, support each other, and share our deepest secrets. We laugh, joke and play and we sometimes cry together. One friend is named Jeff, he is my Facebook Friend. He created a site that shares witty wilderness tips and sayings from his alter ego, 'Ranger Jeff'. The experiences he writes of help you make your camping experience more enjoyable, however they are not recommended by any safety preparedness manual. He makes people smile. This is a valuable type of friend as he can lift you up when you have been let down, and cause you to laugh out loud at his postings. For instance, "Sasquach are outgoing, but camera shy." or "Deer appear gentle and peaceful, but given the chance will tease Elk." He touches many with his humor and blesses their lives.

God is one of our very best friends also, and it is said he sticks closer than a brother. Make him your friend today, he is a great role model and will be ever faithful to you.

Abuse

"Love does no wrong to anyone, so love satisfies all of God's requirements."
Romans 13:10 (NLT)

Violence or abuse of a loved one should never happen, however it does. Both are victims in the relationship. God will heal the physical pain, mental pain, and wounded spirit. Forgiveness will speed the process. No matter what type of abuse is suffered, the scars will disappear. God will comfort the abused and speed the spiritual healing.

The Nightmare
He knocked me down and made me cry
He pulled my hair and blacked an eye
To what did I deserve this action
I always gave him satisfaction.
In everything I said and did
My true feelings remained hid.
For if I let the truth be said
I might as well be dead.
I'd pray for God to make him stop
or make him go away.
Is this the thanks I get for love, honor and obey?
I meant the vow, " Till death us do part."
My love was true within my heart
The day soon came, I said 'No More'
God opened up a secret door
No more heartache, bruises or pain
My life and sanity I shall regain.
(Original by Linda Barrett)

Seasons

"To everything there is a season.
A time for every purpose under heaven."
Ecclesiastes 3:1 (NLT)

God determined our paths before we were born. Everything falls into place just as he planned it, in his time, not our time. Just as there are four seasons in nature that work in harmony, God created seasons in our lives. He is aware of the circumstances, time, and duration of our seasons. Each season has a distinct purpose. We have a season where new things such as relationships begin in our lives. These relationships grow, some last forever and some end when the purpose of the season is complete. In all our seasons God asks that we remain faithful and enjoy our harvest, whether it be a time of joy or a time of heartache and grief. A lesson is always there for us. God's perfect will is completed in our lives through these seasons.

Father, today I give thanks for all the seasons you have placed in my life to allow me to grow in grace. My life has been challenging at times, however, you have been faithfully by my side all the way. I praise your Holy name. Amen.

Grudges

"Bless those who persecute you, don't curse them; pray that God will bless them."
Luke 23:34 (NLT)

Life is short...don't forget to tell those you love that you do...God says it all the time...Don't hold grudges...it does no good, only robs you of your daily joy. Family members have spats and then do not speak for years...emptiness lives in hearts that should be full. Friends disagree on decisions and they sever relationships only to never find that true friendship again. Do things always go the way they should? No. So always keep your eyes on Jesus and avoid the miseries of the world you live in. Even Jesus said... "Father, forgive them for they know not what they do." (Luke 23:34) Jesus forgave everything BIG... so you can forgive something LITTLE like a disagreement.. Have a blessed day my friends and family and walk in sunshine.

My Father, I love you. You are precious to me today, tomorrow and always. Please don't ever forget how much I love you! Help me to forgive all the little things that upset me and remind me that anything that upsets me is little. Amen.

Somebody's Watching Me

"He will not let your foot slip—he who watches over you will not slumber."
Psalm 121:3 (NIV)

God keeps his eyes on us and so does the rest of the world. As Christians we are held to a higher standard. We are morally and ethically bound to do the right thing and avoid sin. We should practice what we preach and gladly do so. We are not perfect, we struggle with emotions and temptations. We fail and ask forgiveness knowing God forgives the sinner and hates the sin. We want our friends to see a picture of Christ in us and in our actions. It all goes back to the simple rule of choices, you either live right or you don't. Our actions are telling a story, even though we do not say a word. Be sure you are painting an accurate picture for all to see.

Lord, you know our inadequacies. Please speak to me through the Holy Spirit to show respect and love in my life and to others. Let your light always shine through me. When temptations arise, let me feel your presence and be led to make the proper decision. In Jesus' name. Amen.

Your Savior Really Does Forgive You

"He is the sacrifice for our sins. He takes away not only our sins but the sins of all the world." 1 John 2:2 (NLT)

Have you ever thought that your sins were so horrible that even God wouldn't forgive you? Well…the Bible tells us that is NOT true. As much pain as Christ suffered for us, and with the humiliation thrown upon him, Christ still had enough strength as he was hanging from the cross to forgive the thief beside him. This proves to us that He is the most loving and courageous person who ever lived. This proves that you and I don't have a sin big enough that he can't forgive.

Precious Heavenly Father, you are my rock and my salvation. I am grateful and humbled that you took our sins away. Lord my love will heighten with every day I walk with you. Thank you for blessing me and let me continue to be a blessing to others. Amen.

Downward Spiral....

**"For everything that was written in the past was written to teach us, so that through endurance and the encouragement of the Scriptures we might have hope."
Romans 15:4 (NIV)**

When you are in a downward spiral...pray for a short trip! Life can be challenging at times due to sickness, finances, loneliness, and a multitude of other factors. The pits of despair come closer and closer as you slide down the spiral. Sometimes all you can do is fasten your seatbelt as you feel there is no solution in sight. In reality, you are the only one that can stop this spiral. At these times, stop looking down and look up, Jesus is there offering his hand to pull you out.

Dear Lord, I humbly kneel at your feet, giving thanks for all the blessings you have bestowed upon me. Help me now Lord, out of this emotional low I have fallen into. I do not see my way clear and need you to bring me out. Help me to remember my trials are temporary and I am not alone. Let me get lost in the Scriptures of your Holy word and find peace. Praising your precious name and believing you are moving behind the scenes to help your fellow servant. Amen

Demonstrate Your Faith

"So you see, it isn't enough just to have faith. Faith that doesn't show itself by good deeds is no faith at all, it is dead and useless."
James 2:17 (NLT)

Years ago when I taught Sunday School, I chose to minister about Faith to my class of six year olds. I announced that since it was a beautiful sunshiny day, we should all go fly a kite. The children look bewildered then smiled as I pulled two kites from the closet. After our playtime we all sat down under a tree. I explained that it is hard to define what wind is but we know it is there, as the kite rises higher and higher into the sky. Just like when God works in our lives, we don't always see it but the results of our faith are visible in the words we speak and by our actions. As a Christian, we should be willing to demonstrate our faith on a daily basis. Don't just say it, do it, or others will see through it! We pray, we believe, and displaying our confidence in God's ability to bring the word to fruition is a blessing to others.

God's Voice

**"The voice of the Lord is powerful;
the voice of the Lord is full of majesty."
Psalm 29:4 (ESV)**

Have you heard God's voice? Some say His voice is difficult to hear. Many desire to hear it but few have this personal experience. Others feel they hear it in the wind, by a whisper in the night, a natural disaster, or a joyous occasion. Sometimes we make a rash decision thinking God spoke to us to move in a certain direction, and that outcome does not result favorably. God gives us guidance throughout the Bible asking us to pray, and wait upon him for an answer. As humans we are in a hurry and do not always wait. God's voice is powerful and you will know when it is Him.

Lord, I know your voice is the most powerful voice in the universe. Help me to listen and hear your voice for guidance. The evil one may try to fool me, however you will alert me when he is near. I shall not fall into his snare. Amen.

You Are Valuable

> "What is the price of five sparrows? A couple of pennies? Yet God does not forget a single one of them. And the very hairs on your head are all numbered. So don't be afraid; you are more valuable to him that a whole flock of sparrows."
> Luke 12:6-7 (NLT)

Friendships come and friendships go, this is a part of your life lessons. You are worth more than they were willing to pay, so don't be discouraged, don't be short-changed, you are valuable! God knows your true significance and everything about you, he has instilled his love in your heart. He knows the one that waits for you, so continue down the path and trusting him for all your needs. Many will cross your path but the soul mate for you will arrive when you least expect it. For it is in God's time, not yours. Keep the faith, spread the love, and have a blessed day-- it's the thing to do.

Precious Lord, I am humbled by your word, that you would care for me and value me. Sometimes the significance I place on myself is less than worthy of your love. I trust your precious word and hold tight to your promises. My love for you is more than I can say. Thank you for caring and loving me. Amen.

Tit For Tat

"Beloved, never avenge yourself, but leave room for the wrath of God; for it is written, vengeance is mine, I will repay, says the Lord. ...Do not be overcome by evil, overcome evil with good."
Romans 12:19-21 (NLT)

When other people hurt you, you may want to strike out at them and hurt them back. However be aware that retaliation isn't right, and only makes the situation worse. Tempers will escalate, anger will increase, relationships will be severed, and little will be solved. It is sometimes hard to restrain your anger and forgive the other person for offending you. Forgiveness is the key to healing when you have been wronged. Displaying forgiveness, by turning the other cheek, will release you from the bitterness you may harbor. Place your focus on God, and do not allow anything to snatch you out of his grasp. Move forward in peace.

Help me, Lord, to do things your way and have strength not to want to take revenge. Help me to trust that you will resolve the situation in your own time and in your own way. Help me to remember that the truth will always be revealed and the wicked will not win. Amen.

Walk In Obedience

"If you love me, obey my commandments."
John 14:15 (NLT)

As a child, parents would ask you to obey rules to instill proper principles and help build your character. As an adult obedience becomes an important part of your Christian growth as you will always have laws to obey. Throughout the gospel of John obedience to God is underscored time and time again. Obedience to God shows a level of trust you have in Him, and that you understand he is protecting you. God wants us to maintain an intimate relationship with him by showing special regard for his word. Grow with God daily, read the word, study the scriptures and always follow his guidance.

Thank you Jesus for giving us your commandments to follow. These rules are a safeguard that we will not cause harm to anyone on our pilgrimage through this world. I will lovingly live by your word. Thank you for showing me the wisdom of your precious word. Amen.

Sorrow

"Jesus wept." John 11:35 (NIV)

We all experience sorrow in our lives and sometimes have trouble dealing with it. Whether it be the loss of a loved one or loss of a pet, it is painfully tragic. Sorrow is something we are all aware of yet deal with this grief in many different ways. Some will keep the pain inside and some outwardly will lash out to others in their discomfort. God is always there to compensate for our losses with his promises of comfort, hope, and peace.

Dear God, I know there is no pain on earth that Heaven cannot heal. I call on you today to heal my heavy heart. Cry with me and comfort me, restore my joy. In Jesus' name. Amen.

Happiness

"How beautiful on the mountains are the feet of those who bring good news of peace, who bring good tidings, who proclaim salvation, who say to Zion, "Your God reigns."
Isaiah 52:7 (NIV)

Happiness is an emotion we all search for. Is it a fleeting fancy or a permanent state of being? Joy comes from knowing God and having a personal relationship with Him. So the answer to my question is that it can be both. No matter what happens in our life God offers hope and promise. True happiness is the fruit of accepting Jesus and sharing good news with others. Love one another, be happy today!

Thank you Jesus for your precious voice. We will shout it from the mountains and the valleys praising your name. Our Lord reigns. Hallelujah. Amen.

Let Your Spirit Shine

"Do you not know that your body is a temple of the Holy Spirit, who is in you, whom you have received from God? You are not your own; you were bought at a price."
1 Corinthians 6:19-20 (NIV)

Your body is the temple of the Holy Spirit. Genuine Christians will experience this astonishing occurrence. God wants us to know that it is important to care for the Temple of your body. A beautiful body may be attractive, but it is the light inside that will touch many hearts. God clearly states that we are not our own, we are bound to him and always accountable. Men and women should be careful not to defile their bodies by their own lust, or the lust of others. Let's be candid, at times frailty finds us and we think about committing sin. The desire of lust is strong and if we consider committing sin, we should consider the eternal consequence as well. Always ask for forgiveness and remove yourself from situations that may lead you into sin.

Heavenly Father, I thank you today that Your Holy Spirit lives in my body, making it a temple of the spirit. I confess that I may have misused and neglected it. When I am weak and tempted to sin, I pray that your spirit will speak to me and that I will have the strength to turn away. Thank you Jesus for listening to me. Amen

Sin, Oops I Did It again.

"But if we confess our sins to him, he is faithful and just to forgive us and cleanse us from every wrong."
1 John 1:9 (NLT)

OK, who hasn't? The awesome promise God has given us is that HE will forgive our sin, no matter how little or how big. Amen. Some people find the word sin offensive, God finds the action offensive, yet he is forgiving of it. "Go and sin no more" comes from his lips to our ears. If you are conscious of your sin that is a good indicator that the Holy Spirit is in your life. Sin is a problem in all our lives, and deadly to our spiritual health, not to mention how it grieves our Father. Ask for forgiveness and turn away from sin.

Thank you precious Lord for your incredible mercy and forgiveness. Amen.

Imperfect Perfection

"If you are kind only to your friends, how are you different than everyone else? Even pagans do that. But you are to be perfect, even as your father in heaven is perfect."
Matthew 5:47-48 (NLT)

The most crucial thing in life is to be in good moral standing with God. We read that we should all be right with God, but just how right is right? How do we stand right with God? Is perfect righteousness enough? Should we strive for perfection and settle for nothing less? Jesus stated his disciples were to be 'perfect.' Perfection in the dictionary has several different meanings, such as: somebody or something that reaches the highest attainable standard, being complete or without defect, sinless. Perfection is a hard state to achieve, and even if reached does not assure you of a problem free existence. Look at Jesus, he was perfect, never sinned, and his life was besieged with problems. Commitment is more what we should strive for. Live with a devotion or dedication to a realistically sin free life.

Lord, help me be the servant you wish me to be. I may fail miserably, however I constantly strive to be the best that I can be and sin free. You live in me and help me to walk through the hard times with my head held high. Thank you for forgiveness and love. Amen.

Just Say No

"Do not be anxious about anything, but in everything by prayer and petition with thanksgiving present your requests to God."
Philippians 4:6 (NIV)

Often you find yourself doing what others want you to do, or act and behave as others feel you should. Don't be afraid to say no…this is not being selfish. The need to please is embedded inside of us therefore saying the easiest word in the universe becomes difficult. Sometimes we stretch ourselves in our work, our relationships, or just life to the point of nuclear explosion. The answer is pure and simple…take care of you! Respect and protect your personal needs to experience less pressure and more happiness. Focus on the funny side of what is transpiring in your life and remember it could always be worse. The only time you should be overwhelmed is with the grace of God. Pray for God's guidance in all your decisions.

Lord, I know when I am anxious you will send me peace. When I have overextended myself in my commitments I must have the courage to say no to demands of me, just as you answer our requests with a no when it is best for us. Continue to encourage me to make the right decisions, your word is what I will cling to in all that I do. Amen.

All Your Needs

**"And this same God who takes care of me will supply all your needs from his glorious riches, which have been given to us in Christ Jesus."
Philippians 4:19 (NLT)**

As we grow in the Lord we have different requirements. As a baby, baby food was our nourishment, then as a toddler solid foods sustained us. As an adult we can eat steak and potatoes. Our temporary provisions change to meet the requirements of our changing lives. God increases our provisions and always has something better in store. The temptation of sin is ever present in our wicked world. Avoiding the temptation of sin is solidified by absorbing the wisdom and blessings of God's word. God knows our needs and he provides us all the spiritual nourishment we need through His word in the Holy Bible.

Father God, thank you for always providing for me. You are always just and faithful. My future is in your hands and I trust you completely. Amen.

Go Forth And Be Fruity

"But when the Holy Spirit controls our lives, he will produce this kind of fruit in us: love, joy, peace, patience, kindness, goodness, faithfulness, gentleness, and self-control. Here there is no conflict with the law."
Galatians 5:22-23 (NLT)

Fruit grows on trees that have been taken care of through pruning, and spraying during the many seasons. The cultivation of the trees will determine the quality of the fruit.
Followers of Jesus also bear good fruit as they become nurtured in the word. Good fruit does not appear overnight, it can take several years for a juicy apple to mature. The fruit of the spirit also takes time to develop. We should work on the nine qualities God has given us to show ourselves fruitful.

Come Holy Spirit, be my guide. Help me to produce only the best fruit and always keep kindness, patience, and love in my heart. Help me steer clear of conflict. Praising Jesus' Holy name. Amen.

Broken Hearts

"He heals the brokenhearted and
binds up their wounds"
Psalm 147:3 (NIV)

A broken heart causes the most excruciating pain known. This pain is both physical and spiritual. Friends can help soothe the physical pain by being there to show you love and care. When they are gone the pain increases. This pain can be caused by a lost loved one, either through divorce or death, the break-up of a relationship, a son or daughter who has left home, an illness, unemployment, dreams shattered, being shut in, and by alcohol or drugs. Faith in God can help you through these tough times, and friends beside you can support you. If you shut yourself away from everyone, then the only thing that can heal your hurt is the Supernatural Power of the Holy Spirit. God has to take over—making the rainbows appear and wiping away the gloom. Call on HIM for strength in your time of need. Don't try to handle your troubles alone, there is strength in numbers. The comfort is knowing He is only a prayer away.

Precious Lord, when my heart is heavy and my spirit is broken, you will bind my wounds. I have comfort in knowing you will always make me whole. Amen.

Fools Folly

*"Fools think they need no advice,
but the wise listen to others."*
Proverbs 12:15 (NLT)

When we think we are better than everyone else, or wiser than those around us; take stock to see that you are not the one who is blind and foolish. Friends may try to enlighten you about your egotistical ways, take heed and accept the constructive criticism spoken with love. We will sometimes reach a false level of self imagined power, however the real power is in the Love of Jesus and how we demonstrate that love to those around us. Spread the love and make the world a better place, it's the thing to do.

Father God, help me to not be blinded and act foolish. I need to stay grounded and keep my pride in check. Help me to display my love to others and not be boastful or haughty, and to listen when friends advise me. Amen.

Be Cheerful

"The fear of the Lord teaches a
person to be wise, humility precedes honor."
Proverbs 15:33 (NLT)

I try to laugh every day, if not out loud then in my heart. It helps me lighten the load to find something to laugh at when the bottom is falling out of my bucket. I know that worry will not add any minutes to my existence no matter how many ferocious faces I make or drawers I slam. How can I be a good example of a Happy Christian if I don't smile? The blessings God has given me are always a reason to smile as well. I'm forgiven and my sins are covered. Hallelujah!

Lord please help me to be sensitive to others' needs today. When I see them discouraged help me to send a smile their way and cheer their heart. Help me to focus on the many blessings I have in my life and be an example of a contented child of God. Amen.

Kiss It And Make It Better

> "For the more we suffer for Christ, the more God will shower us with his comfort through Christ."
> 2 Corinthians 1:5 (NLT)

Remember as a child mom was the one who could always make anything 'better'? When you were grumpy, out of sorts, or just plain ornery, she would say a word, send a smile, or give a hug and it was immediately better? Jesus is like that, he can bring relief to your hurts and he will do it. His promises will bring you comfort.

Dear Jesus, just wanting to take a moment to thank you for those who are there to make things better when we are disheartened. Our pain and suffering is not in vain. Father, you send such comfort through your son. We are humbled, and praise your Holy name.

Humility

"I have done the Lord's work humbly...yes, and with tears."
Acts 20:19 (NLT)

When we are called to do the Lord's work, much humility is required from us. This is a privilege, not a favor and requires much strength, power, and wisdom that we do not always have within us. God sees our potential and our hearts and we are of great value to Him. Build up your neighbor, stranger, a friend, or family member and do not destroy their sense of self-worth. Think on this... humility is our true strength that reaches into the heavens. Pride on the other hand is a weakness that reaches no further than our ego. Be blessed in the day, love one another, it's the thing to do.

Thank you Lord for all the wonderful things you have done for me. In each beautiful new day you have created, help me to be grateful in it. Help me to be aware of the less fortunate and come to their aid. Help me to be more compassionate of others. Amen.

Patience

"If it seems slow in coming,
wait patiently, for it will surely take place.
It will not be delayed."
Habakkuk 2:3 (NLT)

Patience is a virtue, we want to run, yet it makes us walk. Sometimes my computer teaches me patience. Just like when we pray to God, we want an instant answer. In life we want instant gratification for the work we do. Food is micro-waved in an instant, we react instantly to situations when we should think about our action first. Restlessness is the result of losing tolerance with God while waiting for his plans to be fulfilled. God will always do what's best for you. His timing is different than ours, we just need to trust his judgment.

Thank you Lord for all your blessings. I pray for the patience it takes to wait for the right answer and help me to respond with grace and self-control in all situations. Help me to get out of your way, as you do not need my help. You are in full control. Amen.

Love One Another

"So now I am giving you a new commandment: Love each other. Just as I have loved you, you should love each other. Your love for one another will prove to the world that you are my disciples."
John 13 34-35 (NLT)

"Mom, Sandy is breathing on me... make her stop." I clearly remember these words as a child, my sister would annoy me periodically and I would cry out for help. Mom would answer, "Now, be nice to your sister." I would be fuming as I thought me, why me? She was the one who was being mean to me. Our Father in Heaven says the same thing to us. Love is sometimes hard to do when someone is not acting appropriately. We may think, no way, I don't want to!, or that's not fair! God says do this so others will see me in you. Turn the other cheek. When Jesus was on the cross he said, "Father, forgive them for they know not what they do!" In that respect, it is only a little thing he is asking us to do.

Father, thank you for the blessings you have given to me and help me to remember to love all, even those who persecute me. Guide my lips to say the opposite of what my mind is thinking. In Jesus' precious name. Amen.

Quiet My Soul

"I wait quietly before God, for my hope is in him."
Psalm 62:5 (NLT)

When the world is going fast and you want to go slow… find your quiet place. Ask Him to 'quiet your soul' and give you some peace. Use the power available to us when you sit in silence and listen to God. Always trust God as your foundation and refuge. Times may be hard and many bumps in the road, however God is always our rock and salvation. Listen to the Holy Spirit as it guides you through the day. Do not be distracted, stay focused and on the path destined for you. Have a great day….be blessed.

Lord, show me how to be still and quiet my soul. There seems to be no quiet time in my life as it is so fast paced. Show me where I may change the routines in place to relieve stress and self induced pressure. Help me to learn patience as I wait for your word. Amen.

Healing

"Are any among you sick? They should call for the elders of the Church and have them pray over them, anointing them with oil in the name of the Lord."
James 5:14 (NLT)

I am a very private person when it comes to my health, only my very close friends will know what is going on and sometimes not even them. I believe in the Lord Jesus Christ with all my heart and he directs my steps. I was suffering with severe headaches for several months. These headaches would be sporadic throughout the day and into the night affecting my sleep, my health, and sometimes my attitude. Most people around me didn't notice any change other than the fact I may not have been as happy and cheerful as I normally would. After many doctor visits, blood work, poking and prodding, I was told everything it wasn't however not much of what it was. I finally was diagnosed with a cyst in my sinus cavity and advised to immediately have a biopsy and surgery. I did not accept this route, I prayed and several of my close friends prayed steadily for my healing. I went to a spirit filled church. Members laid hands and prayed on me the night before going to the doctor for surgery. I believed that God is more than forgiveness and saving souls, physical healing is a benefit of atonement. The Scripture I had read and claimed was Psalm 103:2-3 (NIV) which states, "Praise the Lord, my soul, and forget not all his benefits who forgives all your sins--and heals all your diseases." Well long story short, the next day the doctor was shocked…there was no cyst, no tumor, nothing, all was clear. I was tingling from head to toe when I heard that outcome. Praise the Lord, he is still on the throne.

I humbly give thanks to the Lord for his unfailing love. His goodness and mercy go beyond our normal expectations. I walked out on faith believing that he would heal me, and he did. To God be the Glory. Amen.

Signs

"Jesus said to him, I am the way, the truth, and the life. No one comes to the Father except through Me."
John 14:6 (ESV 2001)

In our lives we see signs every day….the Stop sign, Yield sign, Wrong Way sign, One Way sign, etc. We are travelers on our journey to our final home. A lot of these signs we see daily will apply to our journey. We should strive to stop bad habits and not yield to temptation, always right the wrong, and accept that there is only one way to heaven. Once you accept him as your personal savior you are on your way to living eternity with Him. Jesus made a bold claim, as he is the Son of God, and he promised he will save us from our sins, if we choose him. He paid for our sins on the cross. Place your trust in him. One Way never sounded so good.

Thank you Jesus for showing us the sign that leads us straight to you. Amen.

Wrestling With Ourselves

**"For our struggle is not against flesh and blood, but against the rulers, against the authorities, against the powers of this dark world and against the spiritual forces of evil in the heavenly realms."
Ephesians 6:12 (NIV)**

If you and Satan had a match on the Worldwide Wrestling Federation, how many rounds do you think you could go, and who would win? Would you keep up, or hope the referee would send you back to your corner for a lifeline? We deal with spirits of inequity all the time, some we see and others are indiscernible. If we resist the Devil he will flee, so stay strong in the battle.

When believers are involved with spiritual conflicts, the warfare is fierce. We should be prepared with the word of God so that we may maintain our solid ground, His power is in us. Ignorance is no excuse nor weapon against the rulers of the shadows of darkness of this world. Christians must be prepared to wage war in whatever way possible, and as soldiers, our ammunition against the fiery darts are the found in our secret bunker, the Bible! Amen.

Precious Jesus, I know the weapons of our warfare are through you, and you are the mightiest of the mighty. You know the evil one is out to devour as many as he can, as his time is short. Keep us strong in your word and your power to win all our battles. Amen.

The Light Shall Lead The Way

"The Lord is my light and my salvation--so why should I be afraid? The Lord is my fortress protecting me from danger, so why should I tremble?"
Psalm 27:1 (NLT)

Have no fear as you go out in the world...we cannot see what is ahead yet we have comfort knowing our Lord is with us every step of the way. We will always be shown the light when we need it, whether it be about an illness, a decision, or a path to follow. God has our back and is waiting for us to reach our final destination, our eternal resting place with Him! Be at peace, walk in 'sonshine' daily.

Thank you Jesus for your light in my life. I praise your name for every challenge and trial in my path as you always light my life so that I may see a solution. Thank you for holding me close and loving me. Amen.

Thorn In My Side

"You have heard that the law of Moses says, 'Love your neighbor, and hate your enemy.' But I say, love your enemies! Pray for those who persecute you! In that way, you will be acting as true children of your Father in heaven. For he gives his sunlight to both the evil and the good, and he sends rain on the just and on the unjust, too."
Matthew 5:43-45 (NLT)

Once I had a job where a coworker would constantly cause turmoil and grief to me. I finally told her that I would pray for her. She immediately responded, "I don't want your prayers." I answered, "I know, however I'm doing it anyway." That was hard to do because I could feel her dislike every day when I arrived at work. She desperately needed my prayers and did not even know it. Hatred only robs you and the other person of their joy.

Lord, I refuse to allow venomous hate to live in my heart. Help me to be strong and offer hope in prayer to those slowly departing from your grasp due to the lethal effect of hatred and jealousy. Amen.

Unrealistic Expectations

"My soul, wait thou only upon God;
for my expectation is from him."
Psalm 62:5 (KJV)

Once I was planning to visit a new friend in a new city to meet an old friend I had not seen in many years. I made arrangements for the flight and bought some new clothes. I had vacation time approved and was excited for the fun I was going to experience. I purchased some tickets to a show and was elated that the front row was available. I called my friend to share the news only to find out that she didn't share my excitement and just replied with a mere "interesting." No excitement was reflected in her voice, no joy, no happiness for me. I was so disappointed her response was not what I expected, when she was the one who encouraged me to get the tickets. I thought she would be rejoicing with me since we had spoken about attending the show. My balloon was deflated and my bubble was burst. God spoke to me and said… "Don't be sad, something may have happened in her world to give you that response." Although my joy was not hers, I was still happy in knowing that God helped me keep my focus. Our expectations sometimes are unrealistic and we need to remember not to be discouraged.

Lord, help me to realize that not everyone will rejoice in my good news. Help me to be mindful that some people are overwhelmed with burdens in their own lives. My focus is still on you no matter what may appear before me. The disappointments in my life are few and the blessings are many. Amen.

You're Never Alone

**"Never will I leave you;
never will I forsake you."
Hebrews 13:5 (NIV)**

Ever feel like you are alone? Do you need words of hope, just a little something to let you know God is still with you? The Bible states that God will never leave you nor forsake you. He is always there and is speaking to you, sometimes through a brother or sister, Pastor or friend, or even a place or thing. God is just a whisper away. When you were a child you might have thought there was a monster under the bed or something lurking in the dark, and you would call for Mom or Dad to come and comfort you with a tight hug. God will comfort you the same way, just ask him to hold you tight when you have fears. Your Father will give you the peace and comfort you seek.

God is always there to hold you close and love you with his heart and comfort you with his word Softly you hear him in the sun, or in a gentle breeze, so don't be afraid, you are never alone. God is sufficient for all our needs.

The Lord Gives And Takes

"I came naked from my mother's womb, and I will be stripped of everything when I die. The Lord gave me everything I had, and the Lord has taken it away. Praise the name of the Lord."
Job 1:21 (NLT)

We all are aware that the Lord will bless us with many things in our life, but do you ever have the thought that he might snatch them and leave us in poverty like Job thought? When we lose our job, lose our house in a tornado, or death knocks at our door we must remember that God does not want to harm us, he wants us to prosper. There is a temptation to blame God for our losses, but God does not change, he is not fickle, and he does not take back his gifts to us. Who's robbing you? The answer is simple, the thief who comes in the night to steal and destroy. God is a giver, Satan is a taker, and he will try to ruin your life with bad thoughts, and bad actions against you. Give thanks to God for everything that happens in your life and continue to praise his Holy name. The devil has a hefty fine to pay and return everything he stolen from us seven times.

Thank you Precious Savior, that you bless me and watch out for me. No matter what evil may come into my life, I will praise you, for I know there is good in everything you do, even if I do not understand it. Whatever the evil one takes, will be restored, for he is not the one with the ultimate power over me. Amen.

Who Are You?

**"Thank you for making me so wonderfully complex! Your workmanship is marvelous--and how well I know it."
Psalm 139:14 (NLT)**

When people ask, "Who are you?" what do you answer? Your name, your occupation? Normally you would state your name or what you do…however that does not really define who your are. When I was a teen I was the Easter Bunny at church. I would spend the day before filling colorful Easter eggs with scripture and candy for the big hunt. God used his creative genius to instill in me the ability to bring joy to others. Although I was known as the Easter Bunny Lady, I was much, much more… first and foremost a child of the Most High God. Spread the word to those who do not know God, you will be blessed.

Father God, thank you for making me who I am today. My desire to let your light shine through me and bring your Word to others is what I desire to do. Help me to continue to glorify your name in everything I do. In Jesus name. Amen.

Soul Mates

"Is not good that man should be alone."
Genesis 2:18 (NLT)

Romantics all over the world wait for a soul mate to arrive so they will live happily ever after. If we maintain a close relationship with God, I feel he will guide that precise human being to us. A soul mate according to Plato, the great philosopher, refers to a soul mate as a "Pull-apart." A perfect soul was split into a male and a female, and that to be complete, they must find each other and reunite their souls. One may reason that there is one person in the whole wide world that you must find and marry to live happily ever after. As Christians we read in the Bible that God has a divine plan. He knows who your mate is and he will lead you to them. It does no good to say at the altar…tie the knot real tight!! A soul mate is not something you find, a soul mate is something you intentionally and prayerfully become. I feel it is more like a spiritual partner who will grow in maturity through scripture and through the love you both show each other. So, pray believing your mate arrives …however it will be in God's time, not yours.

Thank you Lord for your understanding that it is not good for man to be alone, nor woman for that matter. I am ready and waiting for you to send my soul mate, and ask you be generous with your time. I see you smiling and I thank you in advance for your blessings to come. Amen.

An Ordinary Life

"She gave birth to her first child, a son. She wrapped him snugly in strips of cloth and laid him in a manger, because there was no room for them in the Village Inn."
Luke 2:7 (NLT)

Jesus was born perfect; yet he lived an ordinary life, in an ordinary village, with an ordinary family, and ordinary trade, and he spent time with ordinary fishermen. Yet, as ordinary as he was, when he made the uncomplicated command of "Follow Me" people came. Why? Because those who followed felt his extraordinary compassion. His heart broke for the leper, the woman at the well, and the blind man. See the common thread here? We still follow him today, thousands of years later, with a promise of a Kingdom where there is a magical existence totally opposite of everything we see in this world.

Dear Lord, I pray to you today to have my heart break for those that are in need. Help me to continue to inspire those around me and to show compassion, we should not diminish the light of others. In Jesus' name. Amen

God's Love

"And may the Lord make your love grow and overflow to each other and to everyone else, just as our love overflows towards you."
1 Thessalonians 3:12 (NLT)

Love is the central message of the Bible. Love comes in many different shapes and sizes. Love can be a noun or a verb, as in a feeling or an action. When we give of ourselves to others either by our time or our affection, we are showing love. You might run into a person who does not believe that they are loved by God, that their sin is so horrible that they are lost forever. The Holy Spirit will gently speak to you the words to say to that person. As Believers God's love lives in our hearts and will be shown through our actions.

I pray your day may be filled with God's love and peace, share a smile, someone may be waiting for it. Each day is filled with new blessings, be a blessing to someone. God's love is unconditional, tell others about the love of Christ.

Discouragement

"Be Careful! Watch out for attacks from the devil, your great enemy. He prowls around like a roaring lion, looking for some victim to devour. Take a firm stand against him and be strong in your faith. Remember that your Christian brothers and sisters all over the world are going through the same kind of suffering that you are."
1 Peter 5:8-9 (NLT)

We all grow weary and discouraged and our strength begins to fail. The evil one is there to discourage as he waves relentless attacks against us. We want someone to be there to show understanding, make us smile, and inspire us to continue the walk. Be firm in your stand against the evil one and he will flee. Our encourager is there all along, his name is Jesus. Call on him and he will answer. Feel the warmth of his embrace, he will wrap his arms around you and help you find the way. Be blessed in the day. Love and encourage one another, spread the love, it's the thing to do.

Precious God, you know when I am weary. I long for peace. I give thanks that you are always faithful and ever present in my life. Thank you for your love. Amen.

Anger

"Don't sin by letting anger gain control over you. Think about it overnight and remain silent."
Psalm 4:4 (NLT)

Good morning....there will be times when we don't see eye to eye with another person. Knee jerk reactions and fast biting tongues will cause more harm than good. I have a friend who is quick to anger and it has cost him family members and a wife. Throughout his life he has been a person who angers instantly when criticized or questioned about something that is said. It pains me to see his anguish, however he is not open to discussing any options. Keeping individuals like this in prayer is the only thing to do. God can work miracles where you can only plant a seed. Think about it ....respond with an action not a reaction....have a blessed day, walk in the 'sonshine' of our Lord and Savior...be blessed in the day.

Thank you Jesus that I am able to control my emotions and be slow to anger. Your peace is in me when I hold tight to your word. Place your words in my mind so that I might help another who is struggling with anger related issues. Amen.

Can I Have A Witness

"Go into all the world and preach
the Good News to everyone."
Mark 16:15 (NLT)

Spreading the word can be a tricky situation. For instance, approach someone on the street and you may have a captive audience as you spout memorized words, however you have no reputable credibility. Witnessing should be a display of our Christ-like actions. The words you speak should match the actions in your life. We are to be the light of the world so that non-believers will see something in our gentle nature that speaks to them. Showing your Christianity involves your entire life, not just a few words.

Lord, as I kneel to pray, I know you'll hear the words I say. Help me to be an instrument of your peace and open hearts to let you in. I pray for your guidance. In Jesus' name. Amen.

God's Strength

> "My gracious favor is all you need.
> My power works best in your weakness."
> 2 Corinthians 12:9 (NIV)

Sometimes our strength fails and we grow weary and discouraged. At this time we need someone to come along side us, show us understanding and cheer us up. We need to be inspired to have the strength and commitment to move on. A friend can fill that need and I know that when I fail miserably, God is there to forgive and give me strength. God is our best friend and awaits our cry for help. God will help us cope, place him on speed dial and he is only a call away.

Father God, some days our strength seems to loose its punch and we need a lift. Our confidence may be shattered, and unforeseen things have brought us down. I praise you in times like these for I know all my strength comes from you. My cross may be heavy, but you will never send something we cannot handle. I feel your warmth and your favor is all I will ever need. Thank you for working in my weakness. Amen

Favor Me

"For You, O Lord, will bless the righteous; with favor You will surround him as with a shield."
Psalm 5:12 (NLT)

The glory of the Lord is on you today. Isn't it comforting to know when you walk in the light, blessings will pour down on you? There are no boundaries for God's blessing and splendor in your life. This does not mean you won't have trials or tribulations, but with these burdens God will show you favor. If you think big, God will answer big. The more we please God, the more we will be favored by him with spiritual blessings.

Father God, I praise you and give thanks that your glory is upon me. I am humbled and my heart is filled with your love. Thank you for setting me free and blessing my life. In Jesus' name Amen

Death

"But God will redeem my life
from the grave; he will surely take me to himself."
Psalm 49:15 (NIV)

Death is no respecter of persons…the pain hurts…
it leaves a hole in your heart that heals slowly in time.
Our only recourse is to hold tight to the promises of the
man upstairs…our loved one is now at their permanent
home and we will see them down the road. We are selfish to want that other person to stay with us forever.
God knows when our time is up and he welcomes us
with open arms to start a new journey at our final home.
Death is not the end, but the beginning of eternal life.

*Oh God, the sting of death is mighty to us all. I know
there is no sorrow that heaven cannot heal, and our
loved one is now in your hands, but missed none the
less. This is our temporary home, and our final rest is
with you. Rejoicing that we will see our loved one again
somewhere down the road. Amen.*

Misty Eyes

"Then Nehemiah the governor, Ezra the priest and teacher of the Law, and the Levites who were instructing the people said to them all, "This day is holy to the Lord your God. Do not mourn or weep." For all the people had been weeping as they listened to the words of the Law." Nehemiah 8:9 (NLT)

Powerful sermons always make me cry. The Holy Spirit speaks to me at church services and I am touched in the confirmation that my prayers are heard and answered through His powerful word. The joy of the Lord is your strength. Listening to the word of God is invigorating, and refreshing. The thought that he died for us makes me misty eyed. He can relieve all the hurt, pain, and despair that sin produces and forgive us no matter how big or small that sin may be. All he asks us to do is listen to His word, ask him into our heart and he will live with us forever.

Thank you Jesus for the privilege of hearing your word. Thank you for giving me the strength and direction and motivation to keep moving forward. I will honor you all the days of my life. Amen

Show A Little Kindness

"Your kindness will reward you, but your cruelty will destroy you."
Proverbs 11:17 (NLT)

If you have a loving heart spreading kindness will be effortless. Random acts of kindness are displayed by a person who is of good character, gracious and selfless, a person who thinks more of others than themselves. God sent his own son, Jesus, to die on the cross for our sins so that we might live forever in heaven; this has to be the greatest random act of kindness that the world will ever see. When we take time to pray for others, God pours down blessings on us. Kindness is like a boomerang, it always returns to you. Someone may show up at your door with a surprise of flowers, food, or possibly an unexpected visit from an old friend. That's God. That's good. Praise his name!

Dear God, may the brightness of your glory shine upon us today. On bended knee, I give you glory and honor and thank you for all your many blessings. Amen

Missing Puzzle Pieces....

"For I know the plans I have for you" declares the Lord, "plans to prosper you and not to harm you, plans to give you hope and a future."
Jeremiah 29:11 (NIV)

If you feel like your life is a puzzle and you are the missing piece, or you don't know exactly where you 'fit'... remember these lyrics... "God has got a plan for me...no matter what the circumstance may be." God has the best intentions for you, and he sees the full picture of your life, strife, and blessings. He doesn't want to see you hurt....and you may not understand, however the path is long...keep following Him, he knows the way home. God is in control...so just keep faith in His word.

Father, my complete trust is in you. You are aware of the whole picture and are acting in accordance with it. I am drained, however you will fill me up. Thank you for all your many blessings. I know you will add someone, or something, or an opportunity, or a break at just the right time in my life to make it complete. Amen

My Life Has Purpose

> " If we live, it's to honor the Lord.
> And if we die, it's to honor the Lord.
> So whether we live or die,
> we belong to the Lord."
> **Romans 14:8 (NLT)**

The ultimate goal of the life of a Christian is to uphold the glory of God and to obey his commandments. Everything we do in our lives is to honor His name. Christians are unique individuals, with different qualities of different strengths, dimensions, and unique character. We should live to serve our God, not ourselves. When we 'die' and are born again, we are a new person delighting in the opportunity to live with sins forgiven. We experience a new connection and glorify God in all our actions. Our natural death brings us to our home with Jesus, not an ending, but a new beginning where we were destined all along. Daily search your heart to find ways to be kind to others and help others when a need arises, this will show honor to the Lord.

Father in Heaven, it is my desire to honor you in all I do and say. I thank you for your grace and mercy in my life. I pray that as I live in you and die in you I bring you great honor. Amen.

Guardian Angels

"For he orders his angels to protect you where ever you go. They will hold you with their hands to keep you from striking your foot on a stone."
Psalm 91:11-12 (NIV)

Great comfort can be found by knowing that God's angels are always around you. Angels can appear in the form of a friend, a work of nature, or a stranger. They appear at times of our deepest need and these messengers watch over us. Recently I took a trip to another state to meet some friends. We attended a Sock Hop and while I was jumping and shouting, my temporary cap fell out. At first I was hesitant to speak up. Imagine my despair, in a state far from home, unaware of my surroundings, where would I find help? My guardian angel was not far away, her name was Carol. She offered to drive me to a drugstore to find something to fix the problem. She selfishly left the Sock Hop and her friends to attend to my needs. I found exactly what I needed and the problem was solved. I will always be grateful for my Earth Angel.

Precious Lord, you always know our needs, even before we ask. Thank you for placing angels in our paths to ease our anxiety and pain. Amen.

Loser or Learner

> "Then Peter came to him and asked," Lord, how often should I forgive someone who sins against me? Seven times?" "No!" Jesus replied, "seventy times seven."
> Matthew 18:21-22 (NLT)

We are all sinners. Praise God he forgives! When you sin and try to conceal it from God it only makes your life more miserable. When you confess your sin, He immediately takes it away. Don't think of yourself as a loser, you are in a learning process all of your life, no one is perfect. Alexander Pope, an 18th century poet once said "A man should never be ashamed to own he has been wrong, which is but saying that he is wiser today than he was yesterday." Soap washes away the outside dirt, fire cleanses the inside, and the Spirit of God does both. Don't feel bad, be glad your conscience is still receptive to the word of God.

Thank you Jesus for your forgiveness. Instill in us forgiveness for those who intentionally or unintentionally trespass against us. Turning the other cheek is not always easy, however you have shown us your mercy and we should show others as well. Amen.

Peace

"You will keep in perfect peace all who trust in you, all whose thoughts are fixed on you." Isaiah 26:3 (NLT)

Good morning. Peace is something we all search for. Harmony is peace. Relationships need peace in order to survive. Our relationship with God solidifies when we give acceptance into our hearts. We come before the Father and ask him to cleanse us of our sin and make us new creations...in this we are asking for his peace beyond understanding to fill our hearts. John 3:16 says it all...find your peace today...walk in 'sonshine', love one another, forgive differences, it's the thing to do.

Father God, your blessings bring me peace in each day of 'sonshine'. I bask in your glory and happily await you to show me new things. I love you and your love is stored in my heart to be shared with everyone I meet. You have cleansed me of all my sin and I thank you. I am at peace only by your grace. Amen.

Spiritual Blindness, Paul's Quest

"Listen, you foolish and senseless people who have eyes but do not see, who have ears but do not hear."
Jeremiah 5:21 (NLT)

I have a friend who has been blind for almost six years due to an industrial accident. He may not physically see, but he sees with his heart. He is a very warm and giving individual. He lives in a prison of darkness, in spite of that, his faith is firm as he clings to the light of the world. His sense of humor is intact. He has false eyes and when he places them in the useless sockets, asks: "Are my eyes on straight?, I don't want to scare the little kids." or "If you're scared of the dark…don't go blind." He experienced a period of adjustment and disappointment as he would wake up saying, "Darn, I'm blind" to "Darn, I woke up." What he misses most is the smiles on the faces of his grandkids. Understandably, his outlook on life has changed somewhat, however he faces those challenges in a positive manner. There is a well-known Christian hymn titled "Amazing Grace", it states: "I once was lost, but now I'm found, was blind, but now I see." God has given us all the ability to hear and understand spiritual truths, yet some do not see the benefit, as they are lost in spiritual blindness.

Lord, I humbly kneel at your feet, counting my blessings, with a deep understanding that my life could be changed in an instant. I am blessed to be able to sit at a table of plenty when there are others who have much less. As I face difficulties in this lifetime, please help me not to whine and complain selfishly. Help me to be a comfort to those around me. I am so grateful for your mercy and love. Amen.

Ya Think?

"Whatever is true, whatever is noble, whatever is right, whatever is pure, whatever is lovely, whatever is admirable--- if anything is excellent or praiseworthy-think about such things."
Philippians 4:8 (NLT)

Christians need encouragement every day as we try to remain positive in a negative world. Sometimes we will be dominated by gloomy thoughts about ourselves, others or situations. God has instilled in us mental discipline, we have control over our minds and we can think ourselves happy. We can trust God to take care of any challenge that is before us, worrying and getting upset over a situation will not solve it any quicker. We need to learn not to listen to negative talk from our friends also. Negativity breeds negativity and can only ruin your day, and your relationships.

Heavenly father, I ask that you cleanse my mind of negative thoughts. I only want to think about things that are true, noble, admirable, and praiseworthy so that I may be in peace and reflect your word in my life. Search my heart and rid it of any anxious and negative thoughts, and of any offensive ways. Amen.

Traveling With Happiness

"Dear brothers and sisters, whenever trouble comes your way, let it be an opportunity for Joy."
James 1:2 (NLT)

Happiness can be a passing emotion or a permanent state. Keep feeding yourself with the happiness of the blessings around you, those who know the joy Jesus can bring are alive with inner peace. Happiness comes from knowing not to follow the path of the wicked. Your delight is always in the law of the Lord and on his word you should meditate day and night. So walk in sunshine, God has promised us great things.

Precious heavenly Lord, as troubles surface and may be many, I will look at them with joy. Knowing you are there to help me through these minor inconveniences will enable me to keep my chin up and not be discouraged. Amen.

Who Knew

"For he chose us from the beginning and all things happen just as he decided long ago."
Ephesians 1:11 (NIV)

God chose us in advance to be given an inheritance. We did not have to put on pretty clothes or smother him with meaningless words to flatter and impress. God is a universal mediator and is not restricted to one entity or one group. Every object and happening is under his control and is in accordance with his eternal plan. He is the one that creates emotion in our hearts. Every rosebud, ray of sunlight, blade of grass, and flicker of thunder all declare he is an all present God. Be blessed in knowing that God loves you and I unconditionally. Walk in his 'sonshine' and spread the love, it's the thing to do.

Thank you Precious Lord for choosing us from the beginning. You knew right from the start the path our lives would take. You continually guide us and keep us sheltered from harm. Thank you for your grace. Amen.

Ticket To Eternal Life

"I tell you the truth, he who believes has everlasting life."
John 6:47 (NIV)

There comes a day when we make a choice to turn our back on sin. A void is rooted in our lives that cannot be filled and we become restless. God spoke to my heart when I was nine years old. I asked the Holy Spirit to come into my heart and it was forever changed that day. There was a Baptist church a few blocks away from my house. The nicest lady would come to my house every Sunday morning and walk me and my sister to church. I guess you could say she was a foot soldier for God. She was the Godliest woman I have ever known. She was very influential in my decision to ask Jesus into my life. I wanted to experience a unique relationship she had with him, and I have. Amen.

Heavenly Father, Thank you for your love and forgiveness. I am grateful for the gift of Eternal life. I am in awe of your love for me, and the continued growth in our personal relationship. Thank you for loving me. Amen.

Awakening

"The Spirit of God, who raised Jesus from the dead, lives in you. And just as he raised Christ from the dead, he will give life to your mortal body by this same Spirit living within you."
Romans 8:11 (NLT)

A wonderful thing happens when we accept Jesus as our Lord and Savior, the Bible states that the Holy Spirit makes his home inside of us. We are awakened with a new sense of renewed optimism, happiness, and new dreams. He will energize our dead battery, and send us out on new adventures. Our encouragement comes from the fact our burdens have been lifted and we find strength in the power of God. Find your strength today.

Dear Lord, thank you for your goodness. I am energized by the power of the Holy Spirit now living in me. I rejoice in being able to declare your word and let your light shine through me. Amen

God's Plans

> "Your word is a lamp to guide my feet and a light for my path."
> Psalm 119:105 (NLT)

God promises to prevent us from stumbling, or walking down paths that would bring us to danger. He not only illuminates our steps, he clearly instructs us through the Holy Spirit on decisions we should make. If life suddenly seems impossible, we can hang on to the hope that Jesus will be there every step of the way. We should keep our trust in the one that brings true hope and never give up. No matter how dark it is Jesus will always bring the light.

Thank you Jesus for lighting my path, surrounding me with your precious embrace, and helping my feet to stay firmly planted on the ground. Amen

Death Looks Good To Me

"I believe that I shall see the goodness
of the Lord in the land of the living.
Wait for the Lord; be strong, and
let your heart take courage; wait for the Lord!"
Psalm 27:13-14 (ESV 2001)

Once, when in the depths of despair and walking through a deep depression, death suddenly looked good to me. There were just certain things in life I no longer wanted to face. Financial burdens, loneliness, severed relationships, and illness just seemed to take their toll. I came to the realization that life is a gift from God, and it would be an insult to try to return it, none the less, I was spiritually wounded and had lost all strength. I was crying out for help, yet no one came. The boundaries of my limitations had reached their expansion limit. In this darkness, I cried out to God.

Lord, I know there are no secrets between us. I can honestly come to you with my burdens. When I long for your help I cry out to you. Lift me up Lord, hold me tight and make me whole. Surround me with your precious love and fill me with strength, as the road is long and I am weary. Praising your Holy name. Amen

Getting Lost In The Word

"All Scripture is inspired by God and is useful to teach us what is true and to make us realize what is wrong in our lives. It straightens us out and teaches us to do what is right."
2 Timothy 3:16 (NLT)

Sometimes Christians get disoriented in the literal meaning of the word of God instead of the beautiful words God is speaking to us. They have a perception of living in an unrealistic perfect utopia, when in all actuality we live among imperfect people who are just like us. We breathe the same air, drive the same roads, we worship our creator, we all bleed red; nonetheless, some Christians expect perfection from themselves and others. Flexibility needs to live within each of us, we have decisions to make and we should make those to the best of our training and ability through the leading of the Holy Spirit. We will all make mistakes and stumble. It has been said that God hates the sin yet loves the sinner, think about it. As much as the Bible is a story about God, it's also a story about you, and me, and each and every one of us, as we encounter God in a new way. Will you be the Christian that helps that brother or sister up, or the one that keeps on walking because they sinned and made you angry? Remember to get lost in the word, not the meaning of the word.

Lord, instill in me a tenderhearted attitude toward others. Help me to understand we are not perfect on this earth. Help me to forgive misguided actions of others and of myself. Amen.

Do Not Be Distracted

"Don't be mislead. Remember that
you can't ignore God and get away
with it. You will always reap what you sow."
Galatians 6:7 (NLT)

Do not be distracted by the powerful or the deceitful. Some may have more money, fortune and fame, yet they are not living the life God would want. In this world we sometimes see or know people who seem to 'have it all', but do they? They may be quoting the scriptures, yet living a lie to others and mostly to themselves. Pray for them, God sees all and he is waiting for them to turn around and come back to him.

Dear Lord, I know in you I can safely trust and believe you will keep me surrounded by those who fear you and have a good heart. I pray today for those who believe they are with you, yet are on a different path than the one you have for them. Keep me focused on your word and help me to be an encourager to those who are lost. In Jesus name I pray. Amen.

God's Mysteries

"His disciples came and asked him, "why do you always tell stories when you talk to the people?" Then he explained to them, "You have been permitted to understand the secrets of the kingdom of heaven, but others have not. To those who are open to my teaching, more understanding will be given and they will have an abundance of knowledge but to those who are not listening, even what they have will be taken away from them." Matthew 13:10-12 (NLT)

Do you feel God is a mystery? He has spent considerable time revealing himself to us through his secrets and spiritual truths in the Bible. Mysteries of God are spiritual truths known only by revelation. However, God reveals his mysteries only to those who are obedient to the gospel. In reading the Bible, ask for God's voice to speak to you.

God, your ways are mysterious to some, yet you are clearly defined through your word. The Bible is our guide to you and how we should live our lives. You are precious in our sight, in our worship and in our whole being. I love to praise your name. Amen.

Be Still

"Be still, and know that I am God."
Psalm 46:10 (KJV)

When you are beat up and pounded down by life, or your world may be crumbling down around you, hold on to God's promises. He promises marvelous things are in store. Sometimes when you sit quiet you're able to hear more of what's going on around you. The birds singing, the breeze of a gentle wind, or the laughter of a child, and your own feelings. When you think you have a boat load of problems, don't panic! God is in control and will take care of our problems.

Lord, please forgive me when I try to step in and help you solve my problems. I know you are in control and your time is not my time. Help me to be less anxious in my wait. Thanking you in advance of the blessings you are sending my way. In Jesus' name. Amen.

Harold Be Thy Name?

The Lord's Prayer
Our Father which art in heaven,
Hallowed be thy name.
Thy kingdom come, Thy will be done in earth,
as it is in heaven.
Give us this day our daily bread.
And forgive us our debts, as we forgive our debtors.
And lead us not into temptation,
but deliver us from evil:
For thine is the kingdom,
and the power, and the glory, for ever. Amen
Matthew 6:9-13 (KJV)

Teaching Sunday School to children is a blessing, and joyous event in more ways than one. A young boy in my class volunteered to lead the Lord's prayer. He proudly stepped up to the front of the class and stated: "Our Father which art in Heaven, HAROLD be thy name." I struggled to regain composure and continue with the lesson. Through the years other children would say 'Jesus H. Christ', probably in reference to Harold, or Holy… and in frustration, 'Jesus Pete.' Is this a nonsensical term that has been repeated for years or something worse? Children hear what is said and don't always process it correctly, but rest assured they are always listening to what we speak. Guard your words carefully so that children respect what they say and not take the Lord's name in vain.

My Everything

He is my strength
He is my salvation
He is always by my side
He holds me close
And hugs me tight
He is my morning, noon, and night
In the morning while I'm kneeling
He is ever in my sight
And at noon when I am eating
His praises bear repeating
And when the moon is shining bright
I lift up my heart and take in his light
And sing His praises into the night.

Begin every day kneeling in prayer talking to God and end it the same way. Amen.

Relationships

"Make allowance for each others faults and forgive anyone who offends you. Remember the Lord forgave you, so you must forgive others."
Colossians 3:13 (NLT)

>Relationships are an important part of life. Sometimes they are severed by a huge crevasse which is caused by a situation or misunderstanding which threatens the survival of the relationship. A first move is needed to mend the broken tie, through a phone call, written or spoken word, or an extended hand. The Bible teaches us that sin has separated us from God and our relationship is not complete. God usually makes the first move, he not only extends his hand, but his son Jesus Christ. Do not let ego or pride stand in the way of broken relationships in your life. Take that first step and see that person who offended you in a new light. Bring peace back into both of your lives, God would want it that way. Life is too short to leave open wounds in the hearts of those who were once near and dear to you. Have a blessed day and follow the 'son' love one another, it's the thing to do.

>*Lord, as we deal with our relationships, disappointments, and challenges, bring us to the realization that if something or someone is removed from our lives, that you have something better in mind. Life is not always fair, however you always are! Your love is great and you see the bigger picture for us. Help us to have patience and wait on you. Amen.*

Lying

"If we claim we have not sinned, we are calling God a liar and showing that his word has no place in our hearts."
1 John 1:10 (NLT)

It has been said that Christians believe in God, but not everyone who believes in God is a Christian. A good point to ponder! Sometimes our friends hide behind scriptures and attempt to deceive others into believing that they are holy and above reproach. However, they are not in tune with our precious Lord and Savior. What some do in the name of Christianity makes it difficult for true believers to share the love, grace, and mercy of God with non-believers. When you twist the truth, tell a half-lie so it will benefit you, it is not only hurting you but the one you directed the lie to. A wounded heart is crushed and may throw that person into the depths of despair. Jesus is the Way, the Truth, and the Life, follow him and his direction. We lie when we deceive God, others, or even ourselves. No one should continually have to say, 'Trust Me', their action should stand behind their words. 1 Timothy 4:1-2 states, "These teachers are hypocrites and liars. They pretend to be religious, but their consciences are dead." Take a look at your heart right now, are you right with God?

Heart Health

"If we love each other, God lives in us and his love has been brought to full expression through us."
1 John 4:12 (NLT)

Sometimes it is hard to perceive the moment love begins. I think that a heart can turn a 'just a moment' into 'just a lifetime', just like that. We pray that this feeling will last longer than a moment, a week, or a month. As human beings, we all yearn to fall in love because that experience will make us feel completely alive. Our black and white world is suddenly magnified into one of glorious color. Our euphoric enlightenment is helping us to soar into the heavens. Memories are being made that we will treasure for the rest of our lives. God gives us this same experience. When we turn from our wicked ways and allow Him into our heart, a new love grows. God's unconditional love is one that will never leave us and will grow in our hearts forever. As Believers we are expected to love others. Choose his love for your life today.

Thank you Jesus for your love and for the love in my heart that grows more and more each day for you and for others in my life. Help me to show your love through me to others I come in contact with. Many are hurting and brokenhearted, help me to ease their pain. Amen.

Me Me Me, All About Me

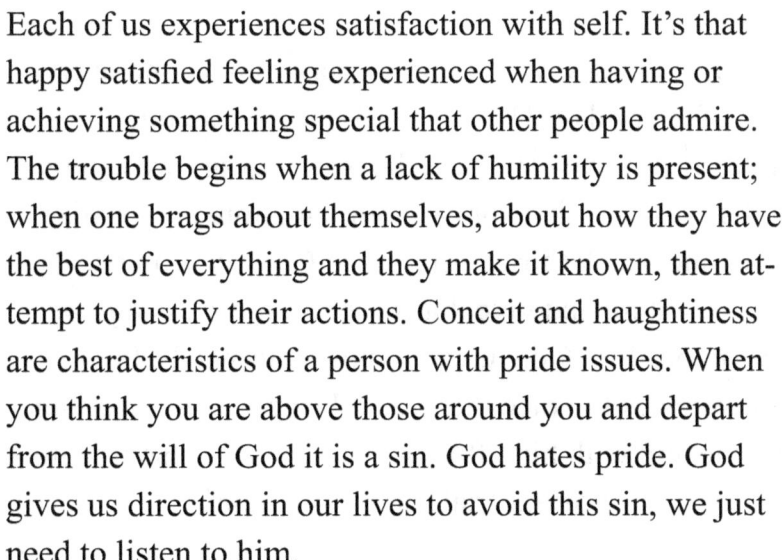

"For the sins of their mouths, for the words of their lips, let them be caught in their pride."
Psalm 59:12 (NIV)

Each of us experiences satisfaction with self. It's that happy satisfied feeling experienced when having or achieving something special that other people admire. The trouble begins when a lack of humility is present; when one brags about themselves, about how they have the best of everything and they make it known, then attempt to justify their actions. Conceit and haughtiness are characteristics of a person with pride issues. When you think you are above those around you and depart from the will of God it is a sin. God hates pride. God gives us direction in our lives to avoid this sin, we just need to listen to him.

Heavenly Father, when my pride stands in my way of real peace for myself and those around me, show me the way to correct my actions to find alignment with God's will and purpose for my life. Help me to shed my stubbornness, and remove my need to be the best in everything. In Jesus' name. Amen.

Precious Prayer

" The deer pants for streams of water,
so my soul pants for you, O God."
Psalm 42:1 (NIV)

Prayer is endless. We can pray every minute and every hour of every day. There is wealth to be found in the Bible, even if we can't find the words to say we can read God's promises that apply to our situation, personalize them, and speak those promises to God. We can simply praise him and give thanks for all the blessings we have in our life. God already knows our needs, but he still wants us to voice them, as it brings us into a closer relationship with him. Prayer is a powerful resource in comfort for all of our trials and tribulations.

Heavenly Father, I believe that there is power in Your Word. Reading my Bible and speaking your word invigorates me. I claim your precious promises and I thank you for increasing my faith every day. In Jesus' name I pray. Amen.

In Everything Give Thanks

" Give thanks in all circumstances,
for this is God's will for you in Christ Jesus."
1 Thessalonians 5:18 (NLT)

So you awoke with the sun shining on your face. You now have two choices, praises to God for the sunshine or put the covers over your head! Always give thanks and praise the Lord for another day that will allow you to be the sunshine in someone else's rain. Many people are struggling with illness or deep despair and only find sadness when they awake. They feel no choices are left for them. God will place these individuals in your life so you may minister to them. Be alert for the signs. Amen.

Thank you Jesus for the blessing of stepping out in another day. Your love is so warm, like the sun, it brightens my day. As I go through my day letting your light shine through me help me to be a blessing in someone else's life. Amen.

Believe

"For I am not ashamed of this Good News about Christ. It is the power of God at work, saving everyone who believes-- Jews first and also Gentiles. This Good News shows how God makes people right in his sight. This is accomplished from start to finish by faith. As the Scriptures say, "It is through faith that a righteous person has life."
Romans 1:17 (NLT)

Can you believe in something you don't see. This is a logical question, however when it comes to God, how can you not believe?. Who else would be a good candidate to trust with your lives and your future? When we go to the Doctor and he says a shot will make us better, we have faith that this professional is being truthful even though we don't know what ingredients are in the shot. When we have faith in God we believe that the Bible is His true word. We have faith that he loves us and only wants the best for us, by setting up guidelines to follow so that we will spend eternity with him.

Lord as I move forward in my journey, I pray for your presence to continue to guide me in what steps I should take. I believe in you from the depths of my soul and I give thanks for your precious love. Amen.

Focus

"Sensible people keep their eyes glued on wisdom, but a fool's eyes wander to the ends of the earth."
Proverbs 17:24 (NLT)

You should focus on your dreams…not your fantasies. Dreams keep you motivated to reach a goal and give you hope for the future. Chasing fantasies is a folly not worth the effort. God has his plan for you. The Bible speaks of being honest, having wisdom, showing love to everyone, and having patience as virtues of a wise person. God is waiting on us to come home and be with him, our focus should always be to live a life that will ensure we have real estate on those streets of Gold. Amen!

God in heaven, my focus is clouded when I follow selfish fantasies. I pray you keep me grounded in the thoughts I entertain. My focus should be on you so that I will not loose my way. Help me to show your precious love to all I meet. Amen.

God Is Our Greatest Encourager

"When they were discouraged,
I smiled at them.
My look of approval was precious to them."
Job 29:24 (NLT)

When it seems like the world is against us, and we just can't get a break we need someone who will give us confidence. Be respectful towards coworkers who are having a bad day and do not be offended if you are snapped at, or are cut off at the copier. The inspiration from a pat on the back, a hug, a simple smile, or just having a friend to listen will help. Throughout the pages of the Bible we find instructions for Christians to encourage one another, this is a part of our stewardship. Sometimes depression cannot be avoided, as someone or something will cause you to feel down. God is our greatest encourager, by reading his word you feel comfort. He is always there waiting to make your day better and bring a smile to your face.

Dear God, I thank you with all my heart for the encouragement you give to me. When others offend me you keep the smile on my face and hug me tight. When life is not fair and troubles surround me, you lift me up. I praise you. Amen.

Can You Fix This

"For nothing is impossible with God."
Luke 1:37 (NLT)

As a child, when a toy broke you would run to Mommie or Daddy and cry "Can you fix this?" A frown on your parents forehead would lead you to believe the answer is "No", however the voice from their lips would be, "Yes, I think I can find a solution." Sometimes the answer would be a quick fix, or a replacement toy…but your cry was answered. You always had faith in your parents to be able to fix things. God is a 'fixer' as well, he is an expert at 'fixing' broken spirits. When we feel powerless and all our efforts are in vain, we can always turn to him to ease our pain. He will hear your prayer, just leave it in his hands.

My precious Heavenly Father, I come to you today to not only thank you for the many blessings you pour down on me but to ask you to lift my heavy load. You can fix me and bring an end to my confusion and pain. In Jesus name I pray. Amen.

God Is Love

"As the Father has loved me, so have I loved you. Now remain in my love. If you obey my commands, you will remain in my love, just as I have obeyed my Father's commands and remain in his love. I have told you this so that my joy may be in you and that your joy may be complete. My command is this: Love each other as I have loved you. Greater love has no one than this, that he lay down his life for his friends."
John 15:9-13 (NIV)

I am so thankful for the relationship I have with my God, my family, and my friends. I appreciate all the wonderful people that have come to my world. Being surrounded by loving caring people throughout the day makes me smile. Love can come in many facets, love of friends, love of spouses, love of family units, and love in platonic relationships. Our human nature can easily spiral relationships into those that can cause hurt, and pain to those involved as a relationship escalates downward out of control. Being rooted in the word of God entrusting him for strength will repair the damage. God is in control.

Heavenly Father, I thank you for your love. Please place your love inside of me so the world can see You through me. Amen.

Encouragement

"The way of the righteous is like the first gleam of dawn, which shines ever brighter until the full light of day."
Proverbs 4:18 (NLT)

God has promised the right path when you seek His truth. Stand right with God, obey his commands and seek his way for your life. Decisions will become easier to make with his guidance. His plan for you will be confirmed if you ask him to show you the path you should take. God loves each and every one of us, hold tight to his promises, have a blessed day, love one another it's the thing to do.

I personally pray today for those who have criticized me, accused me unjustly, and those who have hurt and discouraged me. I choose to forgive them. I do not allow others to control my destiny and choose to keep my eyes focused on what God has in store for me. Jesus was probably more criticized than anyone. He did not need to win approval of others, he silently ran the race ignoring those who were jealous of him. God loves you, and so do I.

Tears

"You keep track of all my sorrows. You have collected all my tears in a bottle. You have recorded every one in your book."
Psalm 56:8 (NLT)

I have read that our tears are unspoken words. Usually they are words of hurt due to pain and suffering, hurt feelings due to words or actions of a friend or acquaintance, or the loss of a loved one. God knows our discomfort and hears our cries. Each of us is very important to God, just like any parent, he does not like to see his children hurt. He is keeping track of those times we are mistreated, have shattered dreams, or when we believe that nobody cares or understands our pain. One day He will hold us in His comforting arms and wipe away all our tears. Accept him into your heart today, and spread the love to one another, it's the thing to do.

Father God, although I hurt and my warm tears flow, I know your grace is sufficient for me and in my weakness, you will make me whole. Amen

Worry

"Give all your worries and cares to God, for he cares about what happens to you."
1 Peter 5:7 (NLT)

We all have worries, this is a human trait. We worry about finances, job security, family, friends, relationships, our fate, and decisions to be made. When our loved ones are away we worry about their safe return. This worry is normal and a natural part of our lives, however too much worry can muddy up our mind and cause us to act irrationally. Worry keeps us from feeling the presence of God and grace in our lives. We find rest from our worries when we give up trying to control our situations, our futures, and trust the One who holds our hand.....God is there, he wants you to trust him. Believe in his word and lay your worries at his feet. Have a blessed worry free day, walk in 'sonshine', love one another...it's the thing to do.

Lord, help me not to spend my time in worry. I will bring my burdens to you. You will lighten my load. Amen.

God Is Forever Yours

"I will be your God throughout
your lifetime, until your hair is
white with age. I made you, and I will
care for you, I will carry you along
and save you."
Isaiah 46:4 (NLT)

What an awesome promise our God has given us. Not only will he be by our side forever, he will continue to care for us, even when our hair is white with age! He created us and we belong to him. Jesus said, "In my Father's house are many mansions." In Heaven, as Believers, we will enjoy the fruits of our labors, help build houses, plant vineyards, fly around with angels and sing praises all day.

Jesus, I praise your Holy name and give thanks that you are an awesome God. You protect us from harm on Earth, and promise to take care of us forever. I thank you for the abundance of blessings you have provided for me. I rejoice at the thought of living with you for eternity. Amen.

Don't Give Up

"So don't get tired of doing what is good.
Don't get discouraged and give up,
for we will reap a harvest of blessing
at the appropriate time."
Galatians 6:9 (NLT)

Have you ever searched for missing car keys and then given up in exhaustion? You think you'll never find them, only to sit in the recliner and be poked in the back by the keys? You gave up too soon. If you would have looked in one more location, they would have surfaced. Sometimes when we feel our season is dry and nothing is working out, it is commonplace to think there will never be a change and give up. There are three things that are essential to the success of each and every one of us, the determination to succeed, the will to win, and the desire to achieve our goals however limited they may be. Your provision is always there, just look beyond your minds eye. Don't be lost in self pity, the devil speaks to you with negative thoughts; don't listen to him.

Precious Heavenly Father, thank you for all you have in store for me. Help me not to give up too soon. I may not see the way, however you are making the way. I pray my strength will increase and I will receive the harvest of the blessing you have prepared for me. In Jesus name. Amen

Belonging

"But this is the new covenant I will make with the people of Israel on that day, says the Lord: "I will put my laws in their minds so they will understand them, and I will write them on their hearts so they will obey them. I will be their God, and they will be my people." Hebrews 8:10 (NLT)

We all have the need to belong. We are social creatures and need that sense of acceptance. We belong to God as his children and friends, and the church as believers. We also belong to one another, husband-wife, parent-child, child-child, and friend-friend. Belonging is essential for a sense of security, yet some treat this gift as an insignificant gift and treat others less than we would like to be treated. God loves us all the same, the sinner and the saint…spread the love, and not the hate….it's the thing to do.

Lord, I am honored to be a part of your life. Belonging to your family is the greatest gift I could have received. Help me to guide others to our family where we can all live together in peace for eternity. Amen.

Friend Buffet

"And the Lord replied to Moses,
I will indeed do what you have asked,
for you have found favor with me,
and you are my friend."
Exodus 33:17 (NLT)

What kind of friends do you have? The buffet of friends includes: Fair-weather, Loyal, Casual, Best friends, those who would die for you and many more. The Bible reminds us that some friends stick closer than a brother, and these are ones I seek out. Jesus wants to be your friend also, he is trustworthy on all levels. Friends are special blessings in your life who you can share companionship, confidences, and they are there to lift you up. Jesus is the role model for friends, and a proud example of qualities to look for.

Thank you for being my friend sweet Jesus. Amen.

Prayer

"I love the Lord because he hears my voice and my prayer for mercy. Because he bends down to listen, I will pray as long as I have breath!"
Psalm 116 1-2 (NLT)

God is always listening for our prayer to arrive in Heaven on the wings of angels. He already knows our need and the answer he will respond. As children, our parents did the same thing. They responded to our requests with the best possible answer. Always in our best interest, as they did not wish us to suffer with wrong decisions or actions. Our Father in Heaven is the same way, he does not wish to see us harmed. When we have to wait for an answer we are growing in spiritual maturity. Welcome the wait.

I will love you for all of my days. You are all I want and all I need Precious Lord. I'm lost without you. Thank you for loving me and leading me in the direction I must go. Amen.

Mean As A Second Language

"Those who love to talk will experience the consequences, for the tongue can kill or nourish life."
Proverbs 18:21(NLT)

My cherished friend spoke to me in heinous unkind words, I still tremble when I recall them. Upon hearing the words, my thoughts were; the tongue pierced my heart, I will surly die now. I was devastated and torn to pieces. Words spoken in haste sting and there is no medicine but time and forgiveness to heal the wound. The sin of the tongue is usually triggered by our very powerful emotions that will cause us to do things otherwise we would not do. Words spoken in anger can lead to sin by misuse of the tongue.

My precious Father, I come on my bended knees praying for control of my tongue. Help me to be slow to anger and not say things in haste. If I have an issue with another Christian, I will calmly address it with them after I have thought and prayed about the situation. I will always ask forgiveness. You are always faithful and tenderhearted, keep me on the same path. Amen.

I Can Only Imagine

"And then I looked again, and I heard the singing of thousands and millions of angels around the throne and the living beings and elders. And they sang in a mighty chorus: "the lamb is worthy…"
Revelation 5:11-13 (NLT)

When we have praise and worship service at our church, the voices in the choir are heavenly. I have not heard angels sing, however I am sure they come pretty close. How glorious it will be to praise and worship Him all day long when we get to heaven. If voices are not on the list of things to be made 'brand new', I will be in the back of the choir.

Praising your Holy name and thinking about the warm tears that will be flowing when in your presence. I pray everyone will experience the excitement in Heaven. By glorifying Your name, I am telling other people that I am yours. Your praise will always be on my lips.

The Lord Direct Your Steps

"The Lord directs the steps of the godly.
He delights in every detail of their lives.
Though they stumble, they will never fall,
 for the Lord holds them by the hand."
Psalm 37:23-24 (NLT)

To be godly means that we submit and pursue God. If we are following him we can be sure that we are on the right path and walking in God's will. No matter what trials or tribulations may come our way, God is faithful and will not allow us to be tempted beyond what we are able to resist without providing a way of escape. Walk assured you are never alone and there is someone there to help guide, lift, and love you. Just as you are warts and all.

Lord, teach us all how to be godly people, to seek your will every day. Your word states that you direct the steps of the godly. I trust you to guide me on the journey you established for me and I know that when I get off track, you'll always be there to hold my hand. Give me peace and confidence by reminding me that you are always in control. Thank you Amen.

Give It Away

"And I have been a constant example of how you can help those in need by working hard. You should remember the words of the Lord Jesus: "It is more blessed to give than to receive."
Acts 20:35 (NLT)

When you give more than you receive, whether financially or in prayer for others, your blessings definitely increase. Prayer, praise, and commitment are factors that will always escalate the blessings in your life and the lives of others. Giving more is not just in tithes, but in friendships, relationships, and to the less fortunate. Food banks are filled with donations at Christmas time, however the destitute need to eat year round, not just at Christmas. Some people amass a fortune of materialistic commodities, but rest assured there will be no U-Haul truck showing up at the Pearly Gates with your name on it. If you find yourself blessed with a table of plenty, share it with those who have none. Give, it's the thing to do.

Faith Or Fear?

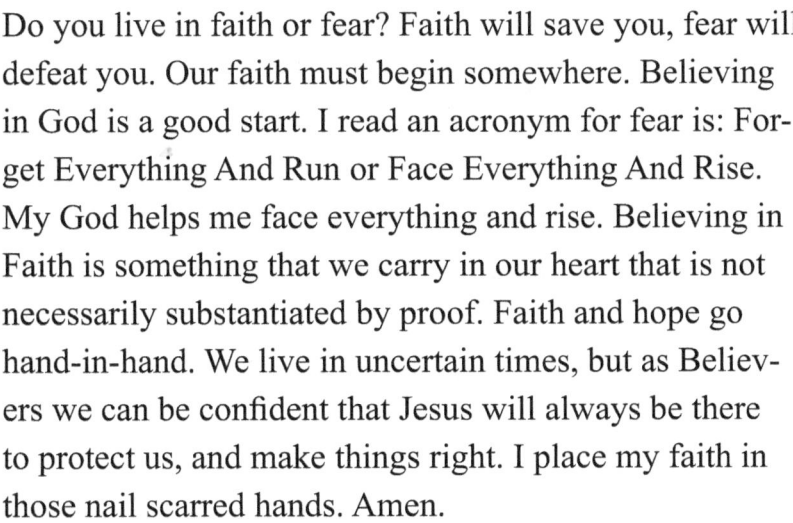

"Faith is the confidence
that what we
hope for will actually
happen; it gives us assurance about things
we cannot see."
Hebrews 11:1 (NLT)

Do you live in faith or fear? Faith will save you, fear will defeat you. Our faith must begin somewhere. Believing in God is a good start. I read an acronym for fear is: Forget Everything And Run or Face Everything And Rise. My God helps me face everything and rise. Believing in Faith is something that we carry in our heart that is not necessarily substantiated by proof. Faith and hope go hand-in-hand. We live in uncertain times, but as Believers we can be confident that Jesus will always be there to protect us, and make things right. I place my faith in those nail scarred hands. Amen.

I praise your precious name that I am able to stand firm in my faith of your higher power. Amen.

Challenges

> "My gracious favor is all you need.
> My power works best in your weakness."
> 2 Corinthians 12:9 (NLT)

As Christians, our lives are not problem free, it seems that challenges are lurking around every corner. Challenges are hidden lessons that God sends to you to make you stronger. We are to be joyful when we meet these trials, as they are developing in you great strength to meet other challenges that will come your way. Our walk with God gives us an opportunity to grow with him as we follow our paths. Being outside our comfort zone helps us listen to the Lord when we are content with our surroundings. When things seem bleak however, the sun always rises to show you a new day.

Lord help me to remember that my challenges are much smaller than my mind makes them out to be. You are able to do all things, and my trust is in you. Amen.

Perception And Reality

"Behold, thou desirest truth in the inward parts: and in the hidden part thou shalt make me to know wisdom."
Psalm 51:6 (KJV)

You may have heard about Punxsutawney Phil Sowerby, he is a groundhog resident of Punxsutawney, Pennsylvania. On February 2 (Groundhog Day) Phil emerges from his temporary home on Gobbler's Knob. If he sees his shadow and returns to his hole, he has predicted six more weeks of winter-like weather. If no shadow is shown, he has predicted an "early Spring." Phil is just a rodent yet year after year people believe his weather prediction. This is proof that perception is not always reality. Satan is very astute at this game of perception, he will have you trembling with fear thinking something is true when it is only a lie. Satan's time is short on this earth and he desires to bring as many people as possible to his final destination. Be alert, when you are fearful of something, assess where the fear is coming from and if it is real or distorted. Ask God for his wisdom to determine what you should do. The Holy Spirit will give you an answer.

Lighten My Load

"But in my distress I cried out to the Lord yes, I pray to my God for help. He heard me from his sanctuary, my cry reached his ears."
Psalm 18:6 (NLT)

In the Bible, there are many times that God asks you to let him carry your burden. He wants you to come to him so that he can energize your spirit, your mind, and emotions. We are only human and can carry so many burdens. How can you witness to others when you are stressed about what is happening in your life? If someone said, "here is one million bucks," you would smile and feel you could soar like eagles. God is always waiting for you to bring your cares and concerns to him, he has promised to take care of you. Let Him bless you with peace and joy.

Father God, I humbly come before you today to relinquish my cares to you so that I may have peace. Help me to find comfort and smile again. Your goodness is overwhelming. I praise your Holy name. Amen.

He Loves Me….
He Loves Me Not….

" For the Lord your God is a
merciful God; he will not
abandon you or forget the solemn covenant
he made with your ancestors."
Deuteronomy 4:31 (NIV)

As a child we have all sung the words of a well known song… "Jesus loves me this I know, for the Bible tells me so." There are numerous scriptures that remind us of God's eternal love, John 3:16 is the most prominent… "For God so loved the world that he gave his one and only Son, that whoever believes in him shall not perish but have eternal life." We all know the Lord is compassionate and gracious, slow to anger and abounding in love. How much more can he love you and me? He wants us to have a loving relationship with Him and to know that he will love us forever without any doubt in our minds.

Precious Heavenly Father, I praise your name and give thanks for the love you have shown to me. Let me be a vessel to share your love with those I may come in contact with. Help me to continually glorify your precious name. Amen

My Constant Companion

"And I will pray to the Father, and he will give you another Helper, that he may abide with you forever."
John 14:16 (NKJV)

My neighbor Wilma is my 'running buddy.' I call her this because every time I say, "I have to run to the store," she is always ready to go with me. She is a great friend and confidant. We share stories about our family, shoulders to cry on, and in lighter moments, laughs galore. When we read God's word, the Holy Spirit becomes our companion and helper as well. A better guide you will not find to teach you, remind you of God's word and give you hope for any situation that may arise. God is my constant companion too. He is always there, always ready to go with me when I travel. Until my forever mate arrives, I am content as I know he is searching for the best partner for me. Amen.

My Precious Lord, I pray to bring me a helper one day. Until then I continue to serve you individually and content in my season. Thank you for the many friends I have that are there to bring a smile, give a hug, or shed a tear. Amen.

Out Of The Dark

"My God turns my darkness into light."
Psalm 18:28 (NLT)

Many people are submerged in spiritual darkness, even though there is light all around them. Believers enjoy spiritual enlightenment while un-believers live in the darkness. Jesus is the light of the world and through him spiritual enlightenment will be obtained. We should be like Paul and lovingly speak to those living in the dark so that they may open their eyes turn away from sin and come to light.

Father in Heaven, I believe in the light, and walk in it daily. Help me to find those who are in darkness, yet are searching for the light so that I may lead them to you. In your Holy name I pray. Amen.

Love Your Neighbor

> " Yes, indeed, it is good when you truly obey our Lord's royal command found in the Scriptures: "Love your neighbor as yourself."
> James 2:8 (NLT)

Your neighbor is not always just the one next door or one who lives on your block. It is anyone you meet. If a need is apparent and you meet that need, you now have a new neighbor and friend! When you share food or clothing with the less fortunate you are pleasing the Lord and obeying his word. Spread the Good News of the Gospel to your neighbor as well, eternal life is a blessing every person needs to be aware of. Spread the love, it's the thing to do.

Thank you Jesus for my neighbors who were strangers that became friends. Help me to extend loving gestures to those I meet and show them the love for you that lives in me. Amen

When You Are Spiritually Stuck

"The Lord upholds all those
who fall and lifts up all who were
bowed down."
Psalm 145:14 (NIV)

Sometimes I get stuck in my spiritual life, I can't seem to get anywhere and the growth stops. Suddenly my enthusiasm is gone and I'm mentally tired. I know what I have to do, but I just can't seem to get there. A hectic schedule could be the culprit. I've been burning the candle at both ends. Sometimes Satan wants to keep us tired and feeling like we're in a rut and going nowhere. When this happens I usually seek help from my church friends; hoping their encouragement and prayers will help me get back on track. I try to think about other things outside of my spiritual life to jolt my mind. I know that in life we have choices, it's either a yes or a no, and negative or positive, but my yes turns to no and my motivation is nowhere. My friend told me that starting is half finishing. That sounded great but it made no change, until I understood what they mean later in life.

I know that I can rejoice when I run into problems and trials for they are a learning experience. I pray Lord that you help me build my strength and confidence and that this bump in the road will not last long. I know how much you love me and thank you for hearing my prayer. Amen

Band Aid

> "And Saul also went home to Gibeah; and there went with him a band of men, whose hearts God had touched."
> 1 Samuel 10:26 (KJB 2000)

God is ouch-less, the band-aid of life that sticks forever and never comes loose. Guaranteed to cure what ails you. Jesus touched many lives as he went along his journey. We read in the scripture above that He touched hearts and those people followed him. We too need to touch hearts and lead them to the one who can heal their pain. Pray that you'll touch a heart today.

Precious Lord, help me to be a band aid in the life of another. Help my kind words of comfort attach themselves to a broken heart, a wounded spirit, or a lonely individual. Some cries are silent, help me to hear those in need. Amen.

Get Right With God

"I am the way and the truth and the life. No one comes to the Father except through me."
John 14:6 (NIV)

Some people walk the straight path, some walk the narrow path, and some choose their own path. This path may give enjoyment now, however ultimately will lead to death and destruction. The path of least resistance is not always the best choice. Choose wisely as your eternity will depend on it. Where is your path leading you today?

I thank you Jesus for showing me the way to you and your heavenly kingdom. I rejoice in knowing eternity awaits me as my path brings me closer to you. Amen.

Birds Of A Feather

"Do not make friends with a hot-tempered man, do not associate with one easily angered, or you may learn his ways and get yourself ensnared."
Proverbs 22:24-25 (NIV)

Companions are important and should be chosen wisely. While on your journey, you need friends who will love you, be loyal to you, advise you wisely, and be positive. God places the right contacts into your life, and you chose some on your own. The choices that you make should be equally yoked. Everyone is not on the same path and God's destination for you may not be where they want to go. Life is too short to spend time with people who are always angry with you, belittling you, telling you what you can or cannot do, or controlling your every move. When you move away from the wrong people in your life God will bring you the right people to take their place.

Lord, thank you for the people you have placed in my life. Your choices are always right. I have faith that if I have chosen someone in my life who is not the best fit, you will reveal that to me.
Amen

Don't Be Offended

"And blessed is the one that is not offended by me."
Matthew 11:6 (ESV 2001)

If you are like most people, you have experienced being offended in one way or another by a friend or family member. Sometimes a misunderstood comment or action will cause offense and wound your spirit. God does not want to see his people hurt. That is why he wants us to keep our eyes focused on him. Holding on to grudges because you were offended does not contribute to your happiness or mental health. Remember these thoughts, do not be offended, do not take things personally, do not frustrate yourself with things that are not in your control, do not lose your peace of mind over little things. Forgive that person and go on your merry way being a true witness to Jesus and knowing that all he requires of you is your love and obedience.

Lord help me to not act or speak harshly to others. If I offend someone help me to realize it and ask forgiveness quickly. Hurt feelings or misunderstandings fester swiftly, help me to do what you have instructed--forgive and move on. Amen.

Why Me

"I love all who love me. Those who search for me will surely find me."
Proverbs 8:17 (NLT)

He loves me like he loves me
and that's all I have to say.
It's never to little
and never too much.
It's just enough to keep me
embraced in his gentle touch.
original by Linda Barrett

As Christians, our lives are not always the greatest, we all experience pain and sorrow like the un-believer. Our saving grace is that Jesus is always just a prayer away. During a season when many possessions were removed from my grasp, He was still there to provide for me. I asked, "Why Me?", and He answered, "Why Not?" He showed me that I could now be an encourager to others who are in a similar situation. Do I always know the right things to say? Absolutely not! However I can be there with a hug, a smile and some encouraging words. We have two choices when life is revolting; be bitter or be better. Through all this my faith in God increased and my faith is something no one can ever take from me.

Lord Jesus, when all I have is taken away and I feel broken down, you are always there to lift me up and take away my frown. For this I give thanks. Amen.

The Object Of Your Affection

**Long ago the Lord said to Israel:
"I have left you, my people, with an
everlasting love. With unfailing love
I have drawn you to myself."
Jeremiah 31:3 (NLT)**

When you meet someone and are attracted to them, you want to get to know them better. You talk on the phone for hours. You make time for them and let them know how much you care for them and the love begins to grow. Communication is the key to make a relationship blossom. God is no different. If we wish to have his favor, we must come to him. We can speak to him in prayer and meditation. We will be able to listen to his word in return. God shows us how much he loves us in the Bible and by his actions. These actions will draw us closer together. We will feel safe and secure with him, and trust him whole heartedly. Just like your physical relationship, you will find yourself spending more time in His word and trusting him more and more.

Thank you Lord for all the little things you send my way to show your precious love. Whether it is just a happy thought, or an individual that makes me smile, it is much appreciated. You make the dark clouds dissipate and the sunshine bright in my day. I praise your Holy name. Amen.

Time Management

"There is a time for everything and a season for every activity under heaven."
Ecclesiastes 3:1 (NLT)

Do you have it? I often hear a common complaint... "I have too much, or I have too little". Sometimes the biggest time wasters are ourselves...we allow 'other' things to get in our way. Work will usually expand to fill our time allotted for it. When is it our time to follow Jesus? Pray for the Lord to open up time in your day to find a quiet place and talk to Him. God gives us time in which to conduct our business, family matters, etc. Some we control some we don't ...like birth, death, the time Jesus returns to us. Use your time wisely and plan ahead. God created the earth in seven days; however you have the luxury to work a little slower.

Lord, give me time. Help me not to be pressured into wasting time due to my lack of planning. My seasons are passing quickly, help me to appreciate the time I have and use it wisely for you. Amen.

Blowing In The Wind

"I love the Lord because he hears my voice and answers my prayers."
Psalm 116:1 (NLT)

A friend of mine, Henry, shared a story to me of a time when he cried out to the Lord in prayer and he received a swift answer. Henry was at Wal-Mart to cash his social security check. He purchased three money orders to pay bills and placed them in his shirt pocket then finished his grocery shopping. As he walked out of Wal-Mart pushing his basket toward his car, a ferocious gust of wind came upon him. He felt papers touching his face but thought nothing of it. He hopped in his truck and went to his next stop. Almost home, he realized his money orders were gone and cried out to the Lord in prayer. He quickly returned to Wal-Mart. The parking lot gave no sight of any money orders so he walked in the alley where employees break to see if the wind had blown them there. Suddenly he saw a piece of paper on the ground, then another, and finally the third money order was located. He immediately gave thanks to God for showing him where the money orders were. We serve an awesome God who hears our prayers and will direct our steps.

Thank you Jesus for being here, there, and everywhere I go. I praise your Holy name for paying attention to my needs. Amen.

Defeat

"This is my command--be strong and courageous! Do not be afraid or discouraged. For the LORD your God is with you wherever you go."
Joshua 1:9 (NLT)

As bewildering as it may seem, feelings of defeat met me as I awoke this morning, however an unpredictable blessing bloomed before my eyes to straighten my path. We are all merely individuals on an adventure through time and space. An expedition of sorts to solidify our place in this universe. We need to lean on each other for security, the word of God for courage and perseverance, and lift ourselves as we encourage those who walk in unison beside us. A morning self talk is always helpful.

I thank you Lord for blessings no matter how small that are available at the exact time of need. Your power is undeniable and you make me strong. I pray I may be an inspiration to my fellow Globetrotters as we follow the path that brings us closer to you. Amen!

Hugs

**"Then he took the children unto his arms and placed his hands on their heads and blessed them."
Mark 10:16 (NLT)**

Can you imagine growing up in a family where no one showed affection? Unfortunately there are many out there. Emotions are not displayed yet are severely needed. I grew up with a girlfriend who was not a touchy-feely type of person. I questioned her about this as when we were in a crowd of people and someone would come to hug her she looked awkward in the moment. She shared that her dad never hugged; in fact she did not remember him even hugging her mother or siblings. A hug is an extension of oneself to the well-being of another. God hugged and welcomed hugs. Hug someone today; it might be the only one they will get.

Father God, thank you for blessing me with your hugs. Thank you for instilling in me a loving nature that is nurturing and able to hug others. The touch of a hug is very therapeutic and brings smiles to others. Help me to share hugs daily. Amen.

No Boundaries For Blessings

*"For I was hungry, and you fed me.
I was thirsty, you gave a drink, I was a
stranger and you invited me into your home."*
Matthew 25:35 (NLT)

A Blessing
When the rug is jerked out from under your feet
And you suddenly have nothing,
Not a mere morsel to eat
You cry up to Jesus through warm flowing tears,
"Oh God you can't hear me?" Is your greatest fear.
"Please throw me a bone, I don't think I can do this
I can't go it alone."
You wait for an answer
Days turn into weeks
Then a blessing appears, bright sunshine at your feet.
Whether it came from a stranger,
Or it came from a friend,
It makes no difference as it altered your end.
It was a thought in the mind and it grew in the heart
Because love is a verb not a noun for start.
It's what you give out, not what you take in
God's love is relentless, no boundaries, no end.
original by Linda Barrett

Moving Mountains

"Because you have so little faith, truly I tell you, if you have faith as small as a mustard seed, you can say to this mountain: "Move from here to there; and it will move. Nothing will be impossible for you."
Matthew 17:20 (NIV)

Nothing is impossible with faith because nothing is impossible for God. Prayer is an important part of your Christian walk. Be in a position for God to answer prayer…being a believer, do not hold grudges against anyone, and do not pray with selfish motives. Trials and tribulations will be ever present in our lives…however with God in your heart all the crooked paths will be made straight. Keep the faith.

Thank you Jesus for your promises. Nothing is impossible with you at the helm, and I believe and trust your word. No mountain will be too big or too strong for me to conquer. All crooked paths will be straightened with your help. Amen.

Got God?

"Many nations will join themselves to the Lord on that day, and they, too, will be my people. I will live among you."
Zechariah 2:11 (NLT)

God created the universe and he lives in my heart. He is omnipresent, which means he is continuously and simultaneously present throughout the whole world and more popular than Wal-Mart! Then why doesn't everyone accept him as their personal savior? I would think that a message of love, salvation and eternal life would be a deal maker. Do they not understand the message? Do they think it does not apply to them? The Bible states that Jesus healed the sick, made the blind to see, and forgave people for their sins. So, who is at fault… God, or man? It is human nature for some people to not take responsibility for their own actions, and lay blame elsewhere. So, in this respect it would be their own fault. Being an un-believer is a bad position to be in. Pray for those around you that have not accepted Jesus Christ as their personal savior. Invite someone to church with you so they may hear the word. The gift of eternal life is there for everyone. Amen.

More Than Enough

"If you have two coats, give one
to the poor. If you have food,
share it with those who were hungry."
Luke 3:11 (NLT)

God blessed you with all your earthly possessions. By sharing those possessions you are a blessing to others, you both profit and it makes God smile. A friend of mine arrived at work one day with a great smile on his face. I asked him what caused him such joy, he replied that he gave his brand-new leather coat just purchased yesterday to a to a person selling newspapers on the corner. "It was so cold this morning and he had no coat; I was glad to help warm him." I understood exactly why he did it. I too had seen that person selling newspapers daily. When I would buy a newspaper I would always give a dollar more, and he would smile real big. "God Bless you ma'am" would be his reply. Don't miss an opportunity to be a blessing to those around you, you'll be glad you did.

Dear God, help me to always look for opportunities to give of myself, my time, and my resources to others. Amen.

Wounded Spirit

"The human spirit can endure a sick body but who can bear it if the spirit is crushed?"
Proverbs 18:14 (NLT)

A wounded spirit is the damaged spirit or a crushed spirit down deep in our soul. There is no physical damage however your thoughts, emotions, and behavior will be different. How does this happen? Usually, negative words, actions, betrayal, broken promises, being discarded are contributing factors. You are crushed and are unable to rise. Sometimes refusing to forgive others who have discouraged and hurt us will lead us to have a wounded spirit that cannot be healed until you extend the hand of forgiveness. The Holy Spirit is therapeutic and will help remove the negativity in your life and assist with your healing. Always pray for the person who hurt you as they may be in pain themselves.

Dear Lord, a wounded spirit can be like death from a sharp tongue or unkind action. I know you heal the brokenhearted, however help me to be cognizant of my actions to not inflict harm or pain to anyone. Amen.

Touch Me

"If you don't touch…you don't feel." Touch has many meanings to different people. Webster defines Touch as: the act of touching, mental or moral sensitiveness or responsiveness, a transient emotion. Touching is capable of arousing emotions or tenderness of compassion. We should all be sensitive to the needs of others. It is a proven fact that touch, either by word or physical attempt releases happy fuzzy feelings inside. Without this connection something dies inside us. Your touch via a hug, a pat on the back, a phone call, card in the mail, or a mere smile is worth volumes to someone who is hurting. Back in the day I would call the operator to ring my number to see if it was working. I accomplished two things, created my own touch and verified my phone was in working order. God can provide that spiritual healing and we must help with the physical part. God has the longest arms of any person I know. He can stretch forth His loving arms around you and bring you under HIS protective care. HE can remove those feelings of failure, depression, and loneliness. We need to make ourselves available to be there to help provide support for those in need. Pray for HIS strength to be made strong in you for those times someone needs you.

Keep on loving each other as brothers. Do not forget to entertain strangers, for by so doing some people have entertained angels without knowing it. Remember those in prison as if you were their fellow prisoners, and those who are mistreated as if you yourselves were suffering.

Lord, I pray for your mighty force to be made strong in me to help others in their time of need. I can always lend a hand or a hug or a smile when I don't know what else to do to comfort a friend. Amen.

What's In A Name

We have many nicknames, given to us from our parents or friends. Some are silly and some are just a shortened version of our given name. For instance, Elizabeth may be known as Betty, James as Jimmy, Linda as Lynn, or Robert as Bob…is doesn't mean we are someone else, we are still the same person. I remember in school some of us would change our names when we had a substitute teacher for giggles and grins…harmless fun that did not last long. Since we were not used to answering to a name that was not our own…the teacher caught on pretty fast. Jesus was known by many names…however it did not matter, as what is important is that we just call on him when we need him. He listens for us to call him, he is aware of his many titles and will always answer. Some of His many titles are listed below.

Christ	Matthew :16
Emmanuel	Isaiah 7:14
High priest	Hebrews 4:14
Good Master	Matthew 19:16
Lord	Romans 1:3
Lord of Lords	Revelation 17:14
Messiah	John 1:41
Prince of Peace	Isaiah 9:6
Son of Man	Matthew 9:6

Lord, I thank you that no matter how we refer to Your Precious Name, that you will acknowledge our prayer and answer us. I am in awe of the many blessings you bestow upon us. I will forever worship you. Amen.

Trust

"You will keep in perfect peace all who trust in you, all whose thoughts are fixed on you."
Isaiah 26:3 (NLT)

Having wonderful friends is one of life's blessings. They stand with you through thick and thin, they are a shoulder to cry on when you need it. You share your stories, your laughter, and your history. "Everyone needs companionship, love, and support in this life." Proverbs 18:24 states: "There are friends who destroy each other but a real friend sticks closer than a brother." Which type are you? Trust in God he will show you the hearts of those around you. Be a loving friend to someone today love one another it's the thing to do.

Lord, I am trusting in you to give me perfect peace. I will keep my eyes focused on you. Great is thy faithfulness, my heart is full with your joy. Amen.

What's Fair Is Fair

"The Lord gives righteousness and justice to all who were treated unfairly."
Psalms 103:6 (NLT)

Fairness includes ensuring that right prevails. We do this when we think of others more than we think of ourselves and we are sensitive to their needs. This justice does not focus on seeing evil or sin win, it is an inner desire for integrity and outward desire to build up self-esteem and others. It is to be like Christ. If someone has offended you, discuss it so that forgiveness may be prayed. God says to forgive others when they have wronged us and for us to seek forgiveness when we have wronged others. This cannot be accomplished if it is a one-sided situation. Share some coffee discuss your concerns and settle any misunderstandings.

Thank you Precious Lord, for your word that when we are treated unfairly you will right the wrong. The flesh is not always filled with integrity. Keep me in your word so that I may know wisdom. Amen

The Yellow Brick Road

"I command you, be strong and courageous! Do not be afraid or discouraged. For the Lord your God is with you wherever you go."
Joshua 1:9 (NLT)

You might be familiar with the Wizard of Oz, a story by L. Frank Baum. A young Lady from Kansas, named Dorothy and her dog Toto were tornado-ported to the fictional land of Oz. Here she met three friends; a brainless Scarecrow, A heartless Tin Man, and a Cowardly Lion who seeks courage. She finds foes from East, and West, then a friendly guide directs her North down a Yellow Brick Road and eventually South, safely home to Kansas. Dorothy met the good, saw the bad, and lived through the ugly. The moral to the story is that you have power within you to be smart, loving, courageous, and strong. Humans are inquisitive creatures. We seem to always search for something we think we can't find, when it was right there all along. Once you accept Jesus Christ as your personal savior, you find that true courage comes from Him, He will direct your path, He lives in your heart, He gives you wisdom through his word, He gives you strength to fight off your darkest enemy, and He awaits you on streets of Gold when you return home.

Lord, I am blessed as when I am disoriented, you surround me with your comforting presence to ease my fears .Thank you for your gentleness and for the hope you give me for the future. Amen.

Broken Hearted

"The Lord is close to the brokenhearted; he rescues those who are crushed in spirit."
Psalm 34:18 (NLT)

Good morning.....God is close and always near even though you may not feel him. When you need encouragement, a little ray of hope, someone shows up to smile, pat you on the back, give a hug, or sit and cry with you. God will never leave you or forsake you. He continually speaks to you through others. Don't miss your chance to be that special someone today. Love one another...it's the thing to do!

Thank you Lord for your comfort and warm embrace. When I am brokenhearted I can find solace in your word that you will heal the pain in my heart. Loneliness and despair are not a challenge for you. I praise your precious name. Amen.

Fork In The Road....

"Show me the path where I should walk,
O Lord; point out the right road for me to follow."
Psalm 25:4 (NLT)

Knowing the scriptures and gleaning their wisdom gives us more options in our decision making and provides us with the discernment we need to make healthy choices. A right decision is one that is consistent with the principles of truth found in God's word. If only one of the opinions would please God, this is the right decision. If there are several options that are consistent with God's Word, then rather than the decision itself, the most important thing may be the process of trusting God to help you make the most of the path you choose.

Thank you Lord for showing me where I should daily take my steps. When I have questions you are always there with answers. Amen.

Burning Bridges

"For if you forgive others their trespasses, your heavenly Father will also forgive you. But if you refuse to forgive others, your Father will not forgive your sins."
Matthew 6 14-15 (NLT)

Good morning. The hardest thing in life is to know which bridge to cross and which to burn. Once a friend asked me if he had burned a bridge; I did not want to hurt his feelings even though he had offended me, so I said no, that he did not. I apologize, that was a lie and I probably did a disservice by keeping quiet...but then if he thought he did and had to ask, I think he already knew the answer. I forgave him and forgot the situation as I knew it would not change the past, however had potential to expand the future. Forgiveness is the ultimate form of love, and in return one receives peace and happiness.

Father, I choose to trust your timing...I believe that you are working behind the scenes on my behalf. Thank you for all the blessings you have in store for me. In Jesus name...Amen.

Draw Me Close To You

**"Draw near to God and God will draw close to you."
James 4:8 (NLT)**

I personally hunger for a closer walk with God and hope you do as well. A True Christian will know the hunger in a heart that yearns for a closer walk with our Heavenly Father. Our Earthly father will hold us tight and build a relationship with us to be there when we need comfort and support. It is the same with our Heavenly Father, he is there to wrap his loving arms around us, to lift us up, to bring us joy, and heal us. You can get as close to God as you want. The Bible states "Draw near to God and he will draw near to you," (James 4:8) this is an invitation by God and he will get just as close as you want him to. He will never let you go. Walk with him daily and the relationship will continue to grow as you mature in His word. Ask him to come fill you up and he will.

Precious Heavenly Father, fill me with your love today and strengthen my spirit. I know how wide, long, and deep your love is. Help me to show that wonderful love of yours to those I meet on my journey. Thank you for the many blessings you have given me. I pray your light will shine brightly through me to others. In Jesus Holy name I pray. Amen

I've Been Robbed

"Go and celebrate with a feast of choice food and sweet drinks, and share gifts of food with people who have nothing prepared. This is a sacred day before our Lord. Don't be dejected and sad. The joy of the Lord is your strength."
Nehemiah 8:10 (NLT)

Do you live in a fast-paced vortex causing opportunities to arise that will cause you to lose your joy? Sometimes we have absolutely no control over the things in our life, but we can always control our attitudes. You rush to work, then rush at lunch, then rush home to take the kids to soccer practice. You are already on edge, then someone asks if you are having a 'bad hair' day, when you thought you were in style.

Guard your joy like you do your wallet or purse. Ask God to bring you a calm and some much-needed peace. The devil knows your weak areas and he roams like a lion waiting to jump in and zap your strength. Jesus gave you the joy in your heart, so Satan can't steal what Jesus gave you in the first place. If you guard your strength the devil will flee. Your joy is a spiritual force and the devil can't get it unless you let him.

Lord, I pray you keep me in check today. I carry your joy in my heart and will not allow anyone to rob me of this precious gift. Amen.

Life Is Like A Merry Go Round

"I am counting on the Lord; yes,
I am counting on Him. I have put my
hope in his word."
Psalm 130:5 (NLT)

Do you just float through a haze some days? Coasting through a period of not making any decisions? No opening mail, no phone calls, a feeling of 'stop the world, I want to get off' is the mindset you are not able to shake? Life may feel like a Merry Go Round at times--getting nowhere just going up, coming down, going round and round and getting nowhere. Don't focus on the success of others, think about all the things God has blessed you with. Discouragement makes us feel sorry for ourselves and the more we focus on it the more discouraged we become. Don't feel like you are the only one sailing through hard times, it happens to everyone. Discouragement is Satan's powerful weapon. Keep focused on the word of God and lay your burdens at his feet.

Keeping Grounded

"Idolatry, participation in demonic activities, hostility, quarreling, jealousy, outbursts of anger, selfish ambition, divisions, the feeling that everyone is wrong except those in your little group, envy, drunkenness, wild parties, and other kinds of sin. Let me tell you again, as I have before, that anyone living that sort of life will not inherit the Kingdom of God."
Galatians 5:20-21 (NLT)

The Bible shows us a guide to be free of the things that may keep us from entering the gates of Heaven. Corruption is in the world and Satan will stir the emotions in us to keep us from the Kingdom. Rest assured that he does not have dominion over us. Conflict may arise, however the Holy Spirit is there to lead us. Be careful not to live in the flesh and be shut out of Heaven.

Lord, please take me by the hand and provide a secure way for me to head into today and all the future days of my life. Guard me from evil and protect my fragile spirit.

What If...Ye Of Little Faith

**"Consider the lilies how they grow:
they toil not, they spin not;
and yet I say unto you, that Solomon
in all his glory was not arrayed like one
of these. If then God so clothe the grass,
which is to day in the field, and tomorrow is cast into the oven;
how much more will he clothe you, O ye of little faith?"
Luke 12:27-28 (NIV)**

Got faith? Do you pray, "Lord, I know how busy you are, but don't forget me, I have a problem." How many times do you start out a sentence with, "Lord, I know you're going to take care of me but if not..." you should be saying, "Lord, I know you WILL take care of me." End of story! If you are like me there have been times in your life when you have worried, you have been fearful, or you have doubted. The disciples also displayed these human emotions so it is par for the course. Faith in God grows as we mature. I am thankful that I have reached a place where I can step out in faith and have no fears, Amen!

Lord, I desire to live a life that is pleasing to you. My spiritual growth is such that the ground I stand on is solid and the hand I hold onto is firm. Thank you for your inspiration, and the glimpses of triumph and peace you so kindly share. I feel the warmth of your embrace and am proud to be your servant. Amen.

Conflict

"Blessed are those who have a tender conscience, but the stubborn are headed for serious trouble."
Proverbs 28:14 (NLT)

Conflict can manifest in two ways, internal and external. Internal conflict arises when we give our lives to follow Christ but cannot disconnect from our old environment. Sometimes it is hard to let go of our old mindset and actions. Tension arises as you battle your choices. External conflict may occur when you have a difference of opinion with another person, usually concerning Religion or Politics. Disagreements will continually happen, the way we resolve these conflicts will decrease the stress involved. Being hardheaded, quick spoken and un-yielding mindsets will cost broken relationships that cannot be mended.

I pray my lips will release words that I have carefully considered, and my actions reflect a faith of true believing. Amen.

Investing For The Future

"Seek his will in all you do, and he will show you which path to take."
Proverbs 3:6 (NLT)

If you want God's guidance you must first invite him in. Direction comes when we seek God's will first. Spiritual understanding is much more than sitting in a pew listening to a few sermons. To fully understand God's word, investment of time and energy and Bible study is required. Commitment to applying your life to the truth you've learned comes next. God sees your heart and your desire to pursue the truth and wisdom. He will open your mind for full understanding and the mysteries of a spiritual life will be revealed. God Bless, walk in 'sonshine', spread the love, it's the thing to do. Think about it.

Lord, when I seek your will, you bless me. I am forever grateful for your mercy. When my goals are met the glory is yours. I know my talents are all from you and I am humbled by your love. Amen.

Lean On Me

"**Never let loyalty and kindness leave you, tie them around your neck as a reminder. Write them deep within your heart. Then you will find favor with both God and people and you will earn a good reputation.**"
Proverbs 3: 3-4 (NLT)

Lean on me is a song that hits home in many ways on so many different levels. "Sometimes in our lives we all have pain, we all have sorrow, but if we are wise we know that there's always tomorrow." Amen! How many times have you had someone say, 'lean on me', and they let you down? God says, you can count on me I will never let you down. He is ever faithful and kind. Friends you choose should also have faithful masses in their foundation and God in their hearts to continually build a sense of security. May your day be blessed with trusted friends.

Lord, thank you for blessing me with trusted friends. My friends are my blessings. I thank you today that you place me in good company. Amen.

Walk A Mile In My Heels

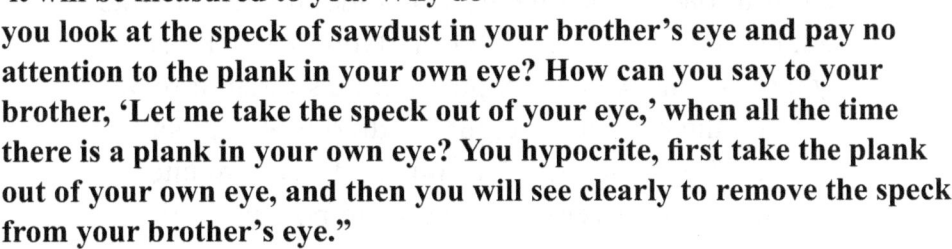

"Do not judge, or you too will be judged. For in the same way you judge others, you will be judged, and with the measure you use, it will be measured to you. Why do you look at the speck of sawdust in your brother's eye and pay no attention to the plank in your own eye? How can you say to your brother, 'Let me take the speck out of your eye,' when all the time there is a plank in your own eye? You hypocrite, first take the plank out of your own eye, and then you will see clearly to remove the speck from your brother's eye."
Matthew 7:1-5 (NIV)

It is plain to see we are not to be judgmental. Our God is a merciful God. He understands everything we do and say. We should realize our own imperfections and refrain from judging others. Don't rely on your own instincts about people, facial expressions, gestures, and behavior may not paint a picture of what's really going on inside their world. Do not be quick to jump with the knee-jerk reaction or quick biting tongue. Make sure you have all the facts, and pray before addressing the issue privately with the other person. And most of all always ask for forgiveness for all involved.

God, construct within me a heart of love and compassion and help me to always consider other people's feelings. I pray for wisdom and discernment. Please help me to forgive my actions, and the actions of others when I become angry when having been treated unjustly. In Jesus' name. Amen.

The Straight And Narrow

"But the gateway to life is very narrow and the road is difficult, and only few ever find it."
Matthew 7:14 (NLT)

There is a road in Canon City Colorado, named Skyline Road, however, I call it the 'O My God' Road. It is a very narrow one way paved, three mile stretch of road nestled on the crest of an eight hundred foot Dakota hogback. This is the most hair raising fifteen minute experience you'll ever have. There are no guard rails, and the drop-off is very steep. It is not advised for those with a fear of heights or prone to a anxiety attacks. When my friends and relatives come visit me, I enjoy taking them there to instill firstly a memorable experience, and secondly to scare the beegebers out of them. It is said you can see dinosaur fossils, however most people just want to see the end of the road. Skyline Road reminds me of the straight and narrow road the Bible refers to. It is somewhat of an unpleasant drive, nevertheless, with a seasoned driver focused on the road, it is achievable. God is our guide to Heaven's gate. He encourages us to walk in Christ, not the flesh and to remain focused on Him in order to find the road without any difficulty.

Lord, keep my eyes focused on you and my walk Christ-like. You are my guide in all that I do and I praise your precious name. The road is narrow and few will find it, help me help those who are searching for the path that leads to you. Amen.

Through The Eyes Of A Child

**"For he satisfies the thirsty and fills the hungry with good things."
Psalm 107:9 (NLT)**

Through the eyes of a child, butterflies, hugs, and kisses are all that is needed. Not much has changed as we grow up. The simple things of life bring great pleasure. Find your contentment, be at peace with neighbors, family, and yourself. Hug one another freely, throw air kisses, spread the love and blessings will abound.

My precious Heavenly Father, I ask that you always allow me to see the view of the world with non-obstructed vision. My wants and needs are not as great as many others, clear away the muddiness of my eyes. May I always rejoice in the rainbow of your precious promises. Amen.

It Is What It Is

"Stay away from fools, for you won't find knowledge there."
Proverbs 14:7 (NLT)

They say one picture is worth one thousand words, but is it? What you see is not always what it is. Just like a peanut in a shell, the inside does not always match the outside. The facts or truth may be covered to appear more likeable to another person. Always listen to your conscience, stay away from deceitful people. God is the same inside and out. You can trust that what you see is what you get, and even much much more! Make a choice, live a lie or walk the truth. Eternity is waiting and you will be satisfied with the results. Have a nice day and remember, we are only passing through so make it a pleasant experience for everyone

Dear Lord, steer my path free of fools and follies. I ask to be focused on you every day and to be aware of those who wish to deceive me. Amen.

Laughter In Heaven

**"The one who rules in heaven laughs."
Psalm 2:4 (NLT)**

Rejoice, leap for joy! In Heaven we will be in ecstasy. No more pain, no more sorrow are two of God's promises that await us when we get to heaven. Now that's joy unspeakable and full of glory to me. I am certain God has a sense of humor cause he made monkeys and they always make me laugh. When you are in a trial or tribulation sometimes humor lightens the situation. I feel the Holy Spirit gives us silly thoughts to help us laugh at life's absurdities and our own humanity. Heaven is a happy place as it means we are finally home!

Dear precious Lord, today I feel your presence and claim the promise that in heaven we will laugh. Thank you for this gift of laughter that we can use freely on a daily basis here on earth to bring joy to those who are hurting and help heal their soul. Amen.

Trust Me

"To you, O Lord, I lift up my soul. I trust in you, my God! Do not let me disgrace, or let my enemies rejoice in my defeat."
Psalm 25:1-2 (NLT)

God cannot lie because he is truth. Prayers are answered according to God's will and we must have faith it will be a positive outcome. Trust God for everything and anything, no matter what the results are, know that his plan is in place for your life. You trust that your sins were forgiven when he was on the cross, and eternal life. You can also trust believing for other circumstances like finances, relationships, and healing. God has given us his promise and his oath and these are unchangeable. When you are in the depths of despair and feel that you are sinking fast, your anchor is Jesus…hang in and hang on. Keep the faith, as a believer you don't always see the outcome but you know there is one. God will never leave you nor forsake you.

Heavenly Father, please see beyond my ways and acknowledge the heart that beats for you. I will trust in your decisions concerning my interactions, my undertakings, and my impending future. Amen.

My Fathers Smorgasbord
My Father.......

Loves me................John 3:16
Cares for me............Matthew 6:26
Forgives me.............Psalm 103:12
Is Compassionate....Psalm 103:4-5
Is Giving.................Romans 8:32
Is Understanding...Psalm 139: 1-2
Is Accepting............Psalm 139:1-6
Satisfies..................Psalm 107:9
Is Reason................Isaiah 1:18
Pardons..................Psalm 103:3
Heals......................Isaiah 1:18
Redeems.................Job 19:25
Is Loving................Psalm 86:15
Renews...................Job 19:25
Is Righteous...........Jeremiah 9:23-24
Is Gracious.............Ephesians 1:7-8
Is Sovereign...........Psalm 103:9

At Random

Rejoice

> THE Lord YOUR GOD IS WITH YOU
> HE IS mighty to save
> HE WILL TAKE great delight IN YOU
> HE WILL QUIET YOU with His love
> HE WILL rejoice over you WITH SINGING.
> ZEPHANIAH 3:17

Rejoice this day that the Lord is with you. Make this day one with sounds of song and laughter. Start the day with a spring in your step, a song in your heart, and a smile on your face. You have much to offer those you meet, as God has built in you a set of special gifts and abilities. Have a blessed day.

I will praise you Lord always. You are God Almighty and no other is like you. Great is thy faithfulness. Amen.

Kindness Nourishes The Soul

**"Do unto others what you would like them to do for you. This is a summary of all things taught in the law and the prophets."
Matthew 7:12 (NLT)**

A loving heart is one exploding with kindness, one of many great virtues. Our society is starved for good deeds. When you water the grass it grows, when you water a soul, it thrives. Kindness is something that we all have inside us, and it is one of the most difficult things to give away as it usually returns to us. We are on this earth for a reason, and that reason is to show the light to those in the dark. Those hurting, those in silent pain, those who have given up hope, water them! God is our greatest model for kindness he sent his Son, Jesus to die on the cross for our sins so that we can share eternity together in heaven. Love one another, hug someone today, say a kind word, it won't cost a thing and the rewards will be incredible!

Dear Father, the golden rule is the simplest guide from your word, yet many seem to have dilemmas following it. Kindness and mercy are traits I wish to exhibit as I journey through this world. Spreading your love is what I wish to do, just as you spread your love to the world. Amen.

Thirst for God

"Hope deferred makes the heart sick, but when dreams come true, there is life and joy."
Proverbs 13:12 (NLT)

In our capacity to desire, which is a trait designed in each and every one of us, we sometimes are tempted to sin. These desires may be Godly, healthy, unhealthy, intense, or persistently casual. The Bible encourages us to develop a thirst for the Lord, to want to know him personally, love him deeply, and desire be close to him at all times. To not be ashamed to share Christ with others, spread God's word, and direct your desires down the path that will honor him. Always strive to walk in the sunshine of our precious Lord.

Lord, you are my life and my joy which grows daily. I am so blessed by your spirit. Continue to fill me with the wisdom that is beyond my expectations. Thank you for guiding me through all my circumstances and keeping me strong. Amen.

Save My Soul

"The Lord will perfect that which concerned me; thy mercy, Oh Lord, endureth for ever; forsake not the works of thine own hands."
Psalm 138:8 (KJV)

There are many unsaved souls in the world around us. God will never force someone to be saved, they have free will to make their own choices, however they cannot escape the convicting power of the Holy Ghost. The Lord knows what it will take to cause someone to turn to Him, no matter how stubborn they may be. We must constantly keep those unsaved in prayer for their salvation.

Heavenly Father, remove the scales from the eyes of those who do not see your grace, and open their ears that they may hear your precious anointed word. Make them aware of your presence and the need to repent of their sins. In Jesus' name. Amen.

Making God Smile

**"Look down on me with love;
teach me all your principles."
Psalm 119:135 (NLT)**

Making God smile is my goal, so that in turn he will smile on me. All of us can make God smile, when we follow his commandments. The only way to Heaven is by accepting Jesus Christ as our Lord and Savior, so do not be confused in the term, to 'please God,' in an attempt to buy your way into Heaven, and the heartfelt motions of our actions. We can be a blessing to those around us by exhibiting kindness, compassion, and generosity. In my senior community I try to always smile to others, and make them smile as well. If I cook too much food, I share with the neighbors, and they return the favor as well. My actions will encourage a joyful attitude and I will rejoice in the fact that I brought good to them and acted in a manner that is pleasing to God. When we do things that are pleasing in his sight, The Lord is smiling down on us.

Thank you Jesus for instilling in me the love that I can share with others. I rejoice that you are in my life and are continually teaching me the right way to live. Amen.

Victory In Jesus

"The Lord, your God will cross over ahead of you like a devouring fire to destroy them. He will subdue them so that you will quickly conquer them and drive them out, just as the Lord has promised."
Deuteronomy 9:3 (NLT)

When you face an insurmountable situation or are confronted with people who use their strength and power against you to frustrate you and steal your joy, God promises he will go before you and destroy the enemy. You will be able to conquer where it seemed impossible, and all with the power of God. Adversaries will become your friends, and doors will open that you can walk through. God always sees the wickedness around you and will protect his servants.

Lord, thank you for your love. You promised you would go before me and make crooked places straight. I know it is never over until you say it's over. Praise your Holy name. Amen.

Count Your Blessings

"For our present troubles are small and won't last very long. Yet they produce for us a glory that vastly outweighs them and will last forever! So all of us who have had that veil removed can see and reflect the glory of the Lord. And the Lord--who is the Spirit--makes us more and more like him as we are changed into his glorious image."
2 Corinthians 4:17-18 (NLT)

Count your blessings in every adversity you face. Trials and tribulations are temporary inconveniences in our lives and we should look at them as lessons to learn from. Our consolation and support comes from the strength and energy we received from God to rise above our challenges. The glory of God is shown to us and to others in all his majesty and holiness. His light is manifested in the gospel to help us see him openly and unmistakably.

Thank you sweet precious Lord that our troubles will be small and will not last long; I stand firm in the belief that you will give us strength to make it through them and see the lesson to learn. You are Holy. Amen.

Broken Dreams

"Bless those who curse you,
pray for those who mistreat you."
Luke 6:28 (NIV)

It is said that we are all 'Born Dreamers'; always find a reason to dream BIG for God. Don't allow someone's words to detour you from your ultimate vision-- keep your focus on our precious Father. Sometimes even as Christians, jealousy will consume a heart and will cause great pain on another person. Spirits are crushed and dreams are broken. A devastating blow that will cause turmoil where no peace remains. God forgives and we should too, prayer is powerful.

Precious Father, help me to remember that you have placed dreams in my heart and will bring those dreams to fruition. Help me to remain focused on you when jealous spirits knock at my door. I believe all my dreams are possible, and trust you will direct my path. Amen.

Listen To Me

"Listen to my counsel and be wise. Don't ignore it. Happy are those who listen to me, watching me daily at my gates, waiting for me outside my home."
Proverbs 8:33-34 (NLT)

Lord, I hear the words you say, now just help me to feel them. Have you ever found yourself in a position where you could no longer feel God's presence? Sometimes we feel like God's peace has left us, we feel a certain void that can't be explained. We no longer feel 'special' and our strong connection to our Lord is not sensed. My experience stemmed from a series of happenings when another Christian wounded my spirit. I felt alone, unwanted, and sad. I did not want to be around people, music, nor attend church. Who moved? It was not God, he was there all along, the evil one placed thoughts in my mind that I was of no value to anyone. I prayed for forgiveness for the situation and forgave the other party. I prayed for God to forgive my thoughts that led me deeper into despair. I kept my faith that God was out there. Slowly I began to feel his presence and feel peace, joy, and my ability to love those around me return. I know I am nothing without the Lord he has said he will never leave us and he does not lie.

Something's Wrong

"Give your burdens to the Lord,
and he will take care of you.
He will not permit the godly to
slip and fall."
Psalm 55:22 (NLT)

When you have a sudden and severe pain what do you do? Most people immediately head for the emergency room as our lives are top priority. When life is not going right-- you can't find or keep a job, finances are in turmoil, family squabbles are escalating, friends are mad, do you head for your Bible or just wait it out to see if it will go away? This is the time you should go to Jesus to help solve your problems. The Bible states "Give your burdens to the Lord." He is giving you instructions so your life will be worry free.

Thank you Jesus for lifting my burdens and answering my prayers. Amen.

You Are My Hiding Place

"You are my hiding place, you will protect me from trouble and surround me with the songs of deliverance."
Psalm 32:7 (NIV)

When I wanted to be alone to think or just relax as a young teen, my hiding place was the big oak tree in my grandmother's backyard. I would grab my transistor radio and climb to the tallest branch and sit there for hours listening to my music. If I was out there too long and it was starting to get dark, my grandmother would be calling my name so that I would come into the house. I would just ignore her because I was happy in my secret place. When I would see her getting close to the tree with that certain look on her face, I knew it was time to come down. Praise God that we have a place to go when we need counsel. We have an owners manual, it is named "The Bible". Any question or concern we have can be answered between the pages of Genesis to Revelation. I am always able to find solutions for challenges there. A quiet place inside or outside with the good book will calm any mountains you are trying to climb.

Dearest Heavenly Father, I give thanks I am your child and you protect me. When I am in my hiding place you comfort me and embrace my soul. I find rest in you and praise your Holy name. Amen.

Eternity Shores…..

"For God so loved the world that he gave his one and only Son, that whoever believes in him shall not perish but have eternal life."
John 3:16 (NIV)

God loves us unconditionally. Does he approve of everything we do…probably not, however he loves us in spite of ourselves. He wants us to come and live with him for eternity. I believe the community will have a huge sign stating : "Eternity Shores" and yes, he planned it for us. What shore will your eternity be found on?

Thank you precious Lord, for all your many blessings. You sacrificed your Son so that I may live with you for eternity. You have taken me from the sad soul I used to be and transformed me into the beautiful creature I am today. I praise you and look forward to being your neighbor. Amen

References

Every effort to locate the owners of all copyrighted material to obtain permission to use the selections that appear in this book was initiated. Any error or omissions are unintentional; corrections, if necessary, will be appear in future editions.

Stories and Quotations
Struggles Of The Butterfly (pg #5)
story from: http://instructor.mstc.edu

Loser or Learner (pg #58)
Quote: by Alexander Pope, an 18th Century Poet
"A man should never be ashamed to own he has been wrong, which is but saying, that he is wiser today than he was yesterday."
www.quotationspage.com

Perception and Reality (pg #99)
Groundhog Day, Punxsutawney Phil From:
Wikipedia, the free encyclopedia

The Yellow Brick Road (pg #125)
Wizard Of Oz Written by Frank L. Baum

Poems
Abuse (pg #8)
by Linda Barrett

My Everything (pg #73)
by Linda Barrett

He Loves Me (pg #110)
by Linda Barrett

A Blessing (pg # 116)
by Linda Barrett

Song References

"God Has A Plan For Me" by Jonathan White, copyright 2004, Jonathan White music.

"Lean On Me" by Bill Withers, copyright 1972, Sussex Records.

Scripture Quotations

(ESV, 2000, 2001) taken from The Holy Bible, English Standard Version, 1999, Tyndale Publishing House

(KIV), (KJB),(NKJB)(KJB 2000) taken from The Holy Bible, King James Version, 1994, Thomas Nelson Inc. Publishers

(NIV) from The Holy Bible, New International Version, 1996, Zondervan Publishing House

(NLT) taken from The Holy Bible, New Living Translation, 1996, Tyndale House Publishers

www.ingramcontent.com/pod-product-compliance
Lightning Source LLC
Chambersburg PA
CBHW062224080426
42734CB00010B/2022